WHEN IN
ROMANS

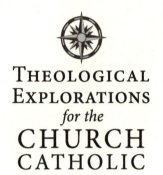

THEOLOGICAL
EXPLORATIONS
for the
CHURCH
CATHOLIC

WHEN IN ROMANS

An Invitation to Linger
with the Gospel according to Paul

Beverly Roberts Gaventa

Baker Academic
a division of Baker Publishing Group
Grand Rapids, Michigan

© 2016 by Beverly Roberts Gaventa

Published by Baker Academic
a division of Baker Publishing Group
P.O. Box 6287, Grand Rapids, MI 49516-6287
www.bakeracademic.com

Paperback edition published 2018
ISBN 978-1-5409-6071-9

Printed in the United States of America

Library of Congress Cataloging in Publication Control Number: 2016010852

Unless indicated otherwise, all translations of Scripture are those of the author.

Scripture quotations labeled NET are from the NET BIBLE®, copyright © 1996–2016 by Biblical Studies Press, L.L.C. http://netbible.com. Used by permission. All rights reserved.

Scripture quotations labeled NRSV are from the New Revised Standard Version of the Bible, copyright © 1989, by the Division of Christian Education of the National Council of the Churches of Christ in the United States of America. Used by permission. All rights reserved.

18   19   20   21   22   23   24   7   6   5   4   3   2   1

In keeping with biblical principles of creation stewardship, Baker Publishing Group advocates the responsible use of our natural resources. As a member of the Green Press Initiative, our company uses recycled paper when possible. The text paper of this book is composed in part of post-consumer waste.

For Matthew, Sarah, and Charlie

CONTENTS

SERIES PREFACE

L ong before it became popular to speak about a "generous orthodoxy," John Wesley attempted to carry out his ministry and engage in theological conversations with what he called a "catholic spirit." Although he tried to remain "united by the tenderest and closest ties to one particular congregation"[1] (i.e., Anglicanism) all his life, he also made it clear that he was committed to the orthodox Christianity of the ancient creeds, and his library included books from a variety of theological traditions within the church catholic. We at Nazarene Theological Seminary (NTS) remain committed to the theological tradition associated with Wesley but, like Wesley himself, are very conscious of the generous gifts we have received from a variety of theological traditions. One specific place this happens in the ongoing life of our community is in the public lectures funded by the generosity of various donors. It is from those lectures that the contributions to this series arise.

1. John Wesley, *Sermon 39*, "Catholic Spirit," §III.4, in *Bicentennial Edition of the Works of John Wesley* (Nashville: Abingdon, 1985), 2:79–95. We know, however, that his public ties with Anglicanism were at some points in his life anything but tender and close.

The books in this series are expanded forms of public lectures presented at NTS as installments in two ongoing, endowed lectureships: the Earle Lectures on Biblical Literature and the Grider-Winget Lectures in Theology. The Earle Lecture series is named in honor of the first professor of New Testament at NTS, Ralph Earle. Initiated in 1949 with W. F. Albright for the purpose of "stimulating further research in biblical literature," this series has brought outstanding biblical scholars to NTS, including F. F. Bruce, I. Howard Marshall, Walter Brueggemann, Richard Hays, Terence Fretheim, and Joel Green. The Grider-Winget Lecture series is named in honor of J. Kenneth Grider, longtime professor of theology at NTS, and in memory of Dr. Wilfred L. Winget, a student of Dr. Grider and the son of Mabel Fransen Winget, who founded the series. The lectureship was initiated in 1991 with Thomas Langford for the purpose of "bringing outstanding guest theologians to NTS." Presenters for this lectureship have included Theodore Runyon, Donald Bloesch, Jürgen Moltmann, Robert Jenson, and Amy Plantinga Pauw.

The title of this monograph series indicates how we understand its character and purpose. First, even though the lectureships are geared toward biblical literature *and* systematic theology, we believe that the language of "theological explorations" is as appropriate to an engagement with Scripture as it is to an engagement with contemporary systematic theology. Though it is legitimate to approach at least some biblical texts with nontheological questions, we do not believe that doing so is to approach them *as Scripture*. Old and New Testament texts are not inert containers from which to draw theological insights; they are already witnesses to a serious theological engagement with particular historical, social, and political situations. Hence, biblical texts should be approached *on their own terms* through asking theological questions. Our intent, then, is that this series will be characterized by theological explorations from the fields of biblical studies and systematic theology. Second, the word "explorations" is appropriate since we ask the lecturers to explore the cutting edge of their current interests and thinking. With the obvious time limitations of three public lectures, even their expanded versions will generally result not in long, detailed monographs but rather in shorter, suggestive treatments of a given topic—that is, explorations.

Finally, with the language of "the church catholic," we intend to convey our hope that these volumes should be *pro ecclesia* in the broadest sense—given by lecturers representing a variety of theological traditions for the benefit of the whole church of Jesus Christ. We at NTS have been generously gifted by those who fund these two lectureships. Our hope and prayer is that this series will become a generous gift to the church catholic, one means of equipping the people of God for participation in the *missio Dei*.

Andy Johnson
Lectures Coordinator
Nazarene Theological Seminary
Kansas City, Missouri

PREFACE

This book on Romans is intended for people who would not normally read a book about Romans. Already there are books—many books—for people who do read books about Romans. Stacks of them arrive on a regular basis. Keeping up with them is nearly impossible, even for the most diligent specialist. As the books pile up, the conversation grows increasingly precise, technical, and challenging for the nonspecialist. And that's a problem, because Romans is too important to be turned over to a handful of specialists, however learned and insightful they may be.

What I have tried to offer in this book is an invitation to Romans, focusing on aspects of the letter that I find crucial, both for the first century and for our own. In the introduction I take up a few general questions about the composition of the letter, but the book is not a survey of the letter. It is also not a commentary on the whole of the letter, although I am preparing one of those as well. I have tried to keep the text itself free of the jargon and the clutter of detailed argument that causes readers to slip away for their siestas. The notes should be helpful for those who want to read further on a particular point, but most readers can simply pass over them. The list of suggested readings at the end also provides an entry point for further study. In the introduction I observe that no one writes alone. Certainly I have not written this book alone. It began with an invitation from Dean Roger Hahn to deliver the Earle Lectures on Biblical Literature at Nazarene Theological Seminary in the fall of 2013. I am grateful to my host and colleague Andy Johnson for the good conversations around those lectures as well as the hospitality extended to me on that occasion. And I appreciate the relationship between the Earle Lectures and Baker Academic, which prompted me to expand and revise those lectures into this book.

I also presented earlier versions of chapters 1–3 as the Currie Lectures at Austin Presbyterian Theological Seminary in February 2015. I am grateful to President Theodore Wardlaw for that invitation, as well as for his friendship of many years. The week itself was a delightful combination of worship, lectures, conversation, and fellowship.

Former students at Princeton Theological Seminary, where I taught courses on Romans regularly for nearly two decades, may recognize anecdotes and analogies to which they were subjected in various pedagogical experiments. With their nods, amens, groans, and even occasional yawns, they helped me sort words that hit their communicative targets from words that needed to be targeted elsewhere. I am happy to acknowledge their assistance.

Friends in ministry Patrick James Willson and Leslie Murphy King read portions of the manuscript and made numerous suggestions for improvement, and I am grateful for their care and encouragement.

Rendering earlier oral presentations into written form became much easier with the help of my graduate assistants at

Baylor University. Scott Ryan and Natalie Webb provided important research assistance at an early stage in the work. Natalie also read the manuscript during the copyediting stage, saving me some embarrassment and making numerous suggestions throughout. Justin King was invaluable in the final stages of manuscript preparation. In addition to tracking down bibliographical information, Justin read the entire manuscript, corrected numerous errors, and became an important conversation partner about Romans in general and this book in particular. I am also pleased to acknowledge the support of the Baylor University Department of Religion, especially our chair, William H. Bellinger Jr.

As much as I might wish otherwise, these fine people are not responsible for the missteps, the infelicities, and the errors that remain in what follows.

This book is dedicated to three people who give me boundless joy: my son, Matthew Gaventa; my daughter-in-law, Sarah Kinney Gaventa; and their son, Charlie. Matthew and Sarah both proclaim the gospel regularly in word and deed, and I hope something here will be useful for them and their congregations. Charlie does not yet read books about the Bible, at least not books without pictures, but I hope he will one day enjoy reading the Bible itself. For now, I am happy to report that this book, although it has no dinosaurs, does have one discussion about trains and the people who ride them.

ABBREVIATIONS

Old Testament

Gen.	Genesis	Song	Song of Songs / Song of Solomon
Exod.	Exodus		
Lev.	Leviticus	Isa.	Isaiah
Num.	Numbers	Jer.	Jeremiah
Deut.	Deuteronomy	Lam.	Lamentations
Josh.	Joshua	Ezek.	Ezekiel
Judg.	Judges	Dan.	Daniel
Ruth	Ruth	Hosea	Hosea
1–2 Sam.	1–2 Samuel	Joel	Joel
1–2 Kings	1–2 Kings	Amos	Amos
1–2 Chron.	1–2 Chronicles	Obad.	Obadiah
Ezra	Ezra	Jon.	Jonah
Neh.	Nehemiah	Mic.	Micah
Esther	Esther	Nah.	Nahum
Job	Job	Hab.	Habakkuk
Ps(s).	Psalm(s)	Zeph.	Zephaniah
Prov.	Proverbs	Hag.	Haggai
Eccles.	Ecclesiastes	Zech.	Zechariah
		Mal.	Malachi

New Testament

Matt.	Matthew	1–2 Thess.	1–2 Thessalonians
Mark	Mark	1–2 Tim.	1–2 Timothy
Luke	Luke	Titus	Titus
John	John	Philem.	Philemon
Acts	Acts	Heb.	Hebrews
Rom.	Romans	James	James
1–2 Cor.	1–2 Corinthians	1–2 Pet.	1–2 Peter
Gal.	Galatians	1–3 John	1–3 John
Eph.	Ephesians	Jude	Jude
Phil.	Philippians	Rev.	Revelation
Col.	Colossians		

Old Testament Apocrypha

Bar.	Baruch	Sir.	Sirach / Ecclesiasticus
2 Esd.	2 Esdras	Tob.	Tobit
1–4 Macc.	1–4 Maccabees	Wis.	Wisdom of Solomon
Pr. Azar.	Prayer of Azariah		

Old Testament Pseudepigrapha

2–4 Bar.	2–4 Baruch	Jub.	Jubilees
Jos. Asen.	Joseph and Aseneth	T. Job	Testament of Job

Other Abbreviations

AB	Anchor Bible
BDF	Blass, Friedrich, Albert Debrunner, and Robert W. Funk. *A Greek Grammar of the New Testament and Other Early Christian Literature.* Chicago: University of Chicago Press, 1961.
BETL	Bibliotheca Ephemeridum Theologicarum Lovaniensium
BHT	Beiträge zur historischen Theologie
BibInt	Biblical Interpretation Series
chap(s).	chapter(s)
ExAud	*Ex Auditu*

ICC	International Critical Commentary
JSNT	*Journal for the Study of the New Testament*
JSNTSup	Journal for the Study of the New Testament Supplement Series
JTI	*Journal of Theological Interpretation*
KJV	King James Version
LXX	Septuagint
MNTC	Moffatt New Testament Commentary
NASB	New American Standard Bible
NET	New English Translation
NIB	*The New Interpreter's Bible.* Edited by Leander E. Keck. 12 vols. Nashville: Abingdon, 1994–2004.
NICNT	New International Commentary on the New Testament
NIV	New International Version
NovT	*Novum Testamentum*
NovTSup	Supplements to Novum Testamentum
NRSV	New Revised Standard Version
NTL	New Testament Library
NTS	*New Testament Studies*
Prot. Jas.	Protevangelium of James
PRSt	*Perspectives in Religious Studies*
Sat.	Juvenal, *Satires*
SJT	*Scottish Journal of Theology*
SNTSMS	Society for New Testament Studies Monograph Series
v(v).	verse(s)
WBC	Word Biblical Commentary
WUNT	Wissenschaftliche Untersuchungen zum Neuen Testament

INTRODUCTION

The title of this book plays on the old saying, "When in Rome, do as the Romans do." That familiar adage suggests that we should behave as the locals do so as not to stand out, not to give offense. Although it sounds like contemporary folk wisdom, it did not arrive in the baggage of twentieth-century relativism. It goes at least as far back as a letter written by Augustine of Hippo around 390. Augustine in turn was citing advice he had received from Ambrose of Milan:

> When I go to Rome, I fast on Saturday, but here [in Milan] I do not. Do you also follow the custom of whatever church you attend, if you do not want to give or receive scandal.[1]

I have transferred the saying, if somewhat artificially, from a place to a text, a very important and familiar text, Paul's Letter to the Romans. And I use the saying by way of introducing the question: What happens to readers, hearers, teachers, and

---

1. St. Augustine, "Letter 54: Augustine gives greeting in the Lord to his most beloved son, Januarius (c. 400)," in *Letters*, vol. 1, trans. Sister W. Parsons, Fathers of the Church (Washington, DC: Catholic University of America Press, 1951), 253–54.

1

preachers of the church in the early part of the twenty-first century, when we are "in Romans"?[2]

My own impression, an impression shaped by decades of teaching in Protestant seminaries and in continuing-education forums of several sorts, is that we are seldom *in* Romans for very long. At most, we make weekend visits. We know the purple passages:

> I am not ashamed of the gospel; it is the power of God for salvation . . . (1:16)

> All things work together for good . . . (8:28)

> Faith comes from what is heard . . . (10:17)[3]

A few more sentences might be added to the list, depending on our particular experiences in Christian communities or our educational backgrounds.

We have probably spent time with the second half of Romans 1 as we discern what Scripture has to say about same-sex relations. We know the closing lines of Romans 8 quite well, because we read them at funerals with hearts overflowing and sometimes even with our fists clenched so that the nails bite into our palms and keep us from losing control. The lectionary may have led us to further study, although I know more than one very fine preacher who regularly opts for the Gospel lesson rather than struggling with Paul's abstractions, with the tortured logic, and with the seeming contradictions in his argument.

2. I use the first-person plural here, as I will elsewhere in this book, not with the notion of coercing readers into agreement but simply in the hope of inviting readers to spend some time in Romans with me. Since readers will bring their own diverse experiences both to reading Romans and to reading my comments about Romans, "we" may find ourselves in disagreement along the way.

3. NRSV. Unless otherwise indicated, translations are my own.

We have read the letter, of course. We have read it multiple times. But that act in itself does not necessarily help, for we read with our predispositions in place. It is as if we ride through Romans on one of those hop-on, hop-off tourist buses, seeing the same highlights every time we travel around the circuit. We never notice that we are in a vast metropolitan area. And that metropolitan area is larger, more astonishing, and more disturbing than we imagine.

In my judgment, that metropolis—large and wild and unsettling—is vital for the life of the church. That is not to say that Romans can be applied narrowly to every issue before us in the church's life. This is not a one-size-fits-all bandage. Romans will not settle the dispute over the color of the carpet or close the gap in the budget. It will not even dictate our music selections. What Romans does, however, is confront us with the universal, cosmic horizon of the good news.

Being "in Romans" for an extended period of time, in the presence of the vastness of the gospel as Paul interprets it, will upset some of our assumptions. As we will see in chapter 1 below, salvation in Romans turns out to involve not just individuals or even groups of people (whether the church or ethnic or other groups) but the liberation of the whole of the created world from the grasp of powers that Paul calls Sin and Death. Chapter 2 takes us into the difficult question of Paul's comments about Israel. There we will find that, especially in Romans 9–11, Paul is less concerned with whether Israel believes in Jesus as its Messiah than with God's unilateral act of creating, redeeming, and sustaining Israel (along with the gentiles). In chapter 3 we take up the question of Christian behavior ("ethics" or "morals"), only to find that in Romans ethics is deeply connected with the worship that all creation owes to its creator, just as worship expresses itself (or fails to do so) with every action of the human being. Chapter 4 concerns the community of believers, which we call the church. There we will see that Paul's comments in Romans elevate believers to the high status of sons and daughters of God, while simultaneously recognizing that the community is capable of severely destructive behavior. At every one of these turns, then, being "in Romans" means seeing ourselves and the world as a whole with disturbing—even brutal—honesty, while also seeing God's action in Jesus Christ to redeem all creation. The universal horizon of the letter does not exist in some strange Platonic realm remote from human struggle; rather, God's universal horizon grasps humanity, re-creating and empowering humanity both for the present and for the future.

Romans as a Letter

When we are "in Romans," we are, first of all, in a letter written two millennia ago by the apostle Paul, about whom we know rather little, to groups of Christians in Rome, about whom we know even less.[4] One of the challenges for many readers of Romans is that it does not much resemble the letters we know.[5] For that reason, it is tempting to read Romans (or other New Testament letters) as if it were a theoretical essay or a treatise rather than a specific word addressed to specific people in particular situations.[6] Especially because it is a letter, however, we need to know something of its circumstances.

4. Paul never uses the term "Christian," and its use is somewhat misleading, especially if it is understood as suggesting that he and other Jewish believers had ceased to be Jews. Yet I find the customary alternatives (e.g., "Christ-followers" or "Jesus-followers") awkward, so I persist in the traditional label, with caution.

5. It might be preferable to say letters as we remember or imagine them, so removed are actual letters from our common experience. For an introduction to letter writing in Paul's world, see H. J. Klauck, *Ancient Letters and the New Testament* (Waco: Baylor University Press, 2006).

6. Even that distinction is misleading, however, since essays and treatises also reflect the circumstances of the writer and her desired audience.

What we know of the apostle Paul comes largely from his letters.[7] Because he is not given to the sort of personal disclosure we have come to take for granted, tracking down information about his life is difficult, and reconstructing Paul's biography is not the task of this book.[8] We do know that Paul has not yet been to Rome, as he indicates in 1:8–15 and again in 15:22–24. That fact seems to influence the letter in several ways. For one thing, Paul cannot appeal to his relationship with these Roman Christians or to their shared experience of the gospel, as he does effusively with the Thessalonians in 1 Thessalonians. He also cannot appeal to any authority he has as the one who first preached the gospel to them, as he does in Galatians and the Corinthian correspondence. He must tread very carefully.

And what can we learn about the audience, apart from the fact that these people also are "called to be saints," as Paul terms them in 1:7, and that they live in Rome? The body of the letter yields very few clues about the audience, and even some of the clues we do find are ambiguous. In 1:5–6, for example, it is unclear whether Paul means that the audience itself is made up of gentiles or that its members live among the gentiles. When Paul writes in 2:17, "If you call yourself a Jew . . . ," does that mean he is in fact speaking directly to Jewish Christians? Or could he be speaking instead to gentiles who have strongly identified with the synagogue? The same ambiguity plagues 7:1,

7. The Acts of the Apostles also contains considerable information about Paul's life and circumstances, but it was written decades after Paul's death, and assessing the historical accuracy of Luke's account is tricky. I advocate employing Acts in a secondary way, as it corroborates Paul's letters, rather than taking Acts as a biographical framework into which to insert bits and pieces drawn from Paul's letters. A classic statement of this problem is that of John Knox in *Chapters in a Life of Paul* (New York: Abingdon, 1950), 13–43.

8. For a brief introduction to questions of Paul's biography, see David G. Horrell, *An Introduction to the Study of Paul*, Approaches to Biblical Studies (London: T&T Clark, 2000); for further discussion, see Calvin J. Roetzel, *Paul: The Man and the Myth* (Columbia: University of South Carolina Press, 1998).

where Paul writes that he is speaking with those who "know the law." Are these Jews, or are they gentiles who have knowledge of the Mosaic law (as in Acts 15:21) or even Roman law? In Romans 11:13 Paul does speak directly to gentiles, but that statement does little to help us determine what proportion of Roman believers were gentiles and what proportion were Jews. The one place where we find specific names is in the long set of greetings at the close of the letter (16:3–16), but this passage also raises many questions about Paul's audience.[9]

The Greetings of Romans 16

Romans 16 does provide us with valuable information about Paul's audience. Yet I suspect many people who read Paul's Letter to the Romans simply skip this last chapter altogether. Apart from the concluding benediction in verses 25–27, the Revised Common Lectionary overlooks this passage, and we can scarcely blame the editors for that decision. When we hit this list of names, we may joke a bit about their strangeness;

---

9. Although other letters do have closing greetings (as in 1 Cor. 16:19–20; 2 Cor. 13:12; Phil. 4:21–22; 1 Thess. 5:26; Philem. 23–24), this is by far the longest list of greetings in any of Paul's letters. Because Paul has not yet been to Rome, it is hard to understand how he is able to greet so many individuals by name. It may be that he greets everyone he knows—even indirectly—in order to consolidate these relationships (so Peter Lampe, *From Paul to Valentinus: Christians at Rome in the First Two Centuries*, trans. Michael Steinhauser, ed. Marshall D. Johnson [Minneapolis: Fortress, 2003], 157). We would probably call it networking. But because he has not been to Rome, and also because there are some important differences among the earliest handwritten copies (manuscripts) of this letter, and even one manuscript that omits the greetings, T. W. Manson argued that the greetings were not part of the original letter. Manson theorized that the original letter to Roman Christians did not have this list of greetings but that later Paul sent the same letter to the Ephesians, greetings included ("St. Paul's Letter to the Romans—and Others," in *The Romans Debate*, ed. Karl P. Donfried, rev. ed. [Grand Rapids: Baker Academic, 2011], 3–15). Most scholars have rejected that theory, because the evidence for it is quite minimal. It seems far more likely that a later editor or scribe deleted the greetings so that the letter would be more suitable for a larger audience.

Tryphaena and Tryphosa are unlikely candidates for popular baby names in twenty-first-century America, although I hope for a surge of young women named Junia. Yet for the most part we breathe a deep sigh of relief that we have—finally—reached the letter's end. This is a bit like coming upon a genealogy in the Old Testament, where we skip over the "begats" and take up the next section.

It may seem surprising to learn that scholars have devoted a great deal of attention in the last several decades to the greetings in Romans 16. Precisely because the body of the letter tells us rather little about the audience, scholars have focused on the greetings in an effort to see what information we might glean from the names themselves. And we know names can reveal a great deal. When I visit the little country cemetery where several members of my extended family are buried, I am sharply reminded that the Scots and the Irish were prominent among the residents of that region for generations. I am not sure there is an Olson or a González buried there, to say nothing of a Cho or a Gertmenian.

This set of greetings reveals several important things about the audience of Paul's letter. First, we should think of it not as a single group, "the Roman church," but as several small groups of believers. Verse 5 refers to the gathering (*ekklēsia*, which we translate "congregation" or even "church") in the house of Prisca and Aquila.[10] Later, Paul greets some individuals by name and then adds "and the brothers and sisters who are with them" or "all the saints who are with them," which could also mean the believers who meet with them.

---

10. For discussion of Christian meeting places, see Edward Adams, *The Earliest Christian Meeting Places: Almost Exclusively Houses?* (London: T&T Clark/ Bloomsbury, 2013); David Balch and Annette Weissenrieder, eds., *Contested Spaces: Houses and Temples in Roman Antiquity and the New Testament* (Tübingen: Mohr Siebeck, 2012).

Second, several of the people Paul greets bear names that were regularly used for slaves, such as Hermes, Nereus, and Persis. Perhaps surprisingly, relatively few of the names suggest Jewish descent. And many of the names are those of immigrants from the Roman East.[11]

Third, a high proportion of women's names appear on the list, and what Paul has to say about them comes as a surprise to readers who have been taught that Paul advocates the submission of women and the suppression of their voices. He comments that Prisca, Mary, Tryphaena, Tryphosa, and Persis "worked" with him (Prisca, v. 3; Mary, v. 6; Tryphaena, Tryphosa, and Persis, v. 12). That bland verb does not convey a great deal in English, but this is the language he uses elsewhere when he is speaking about apostolic labor (as in 1 Cor. 3:9; 4:12; 15:10; Gal. 4:11; 1 Thess. 5:12). In addition, when he refers to the couple Prisca and Aquila, her name comes first, as it does in Acts 18:18, 26 and 2 Timothy 4:19.[12] That is not a gesture to chivalry, since in the ancient world the husband's name usually went first (as in Rom. 16:7; Acts 5:1). The fact that Paul switches the order could suggest that Prisca is the more prominent figure in the Christian community.

Another couple appears in Romans 16:7, Andronicus and Junia. Paul identifies them as "kinfolk," suggesting they are Jews, but he also says that they are "fellow prisoners" and that they are "honored among the apostles." This identification of a woman as an "apostle" was obscured by much of twentieth-century exegesis and translation, which referred to a male "Junias" instead of a female "Junia."[13] Yet interpreters across

---

11. See the meticulous work of Peter Lampe, *From Paul to Valentinus*, esp. 74–76, 164–83.

12. Aquila appears first in Acts 18:2 and 1 Cor. 16:19.

13. The two Greek names are distinguishable in the accusative case, as in Rom. 16:7, only by a single accent mark, and accents rarely appeared in ancient texts.

the first millennium of the church's life consistently identify Junia as an apostle. Equally important, there is no evidence in antiquity for the use of the male name Junias, making it quite likely that Paul indeed includes a woman among the apostles.[14]

Between Paul and Rome: Phoebe

In addition to Paul, the letter writer, and the Romans, the recipients of the letter, there is Phoebe, whose role in the letter's reception at Rome is probably far larger than most readers have imagined. Before Paul greets those who are actually in Rome, he writes a brief introduction for her:

> I present to you Phoebe, our sister, who is also deacon of the congregation at Cenchreae, so that you may welcome her in the Lord as is appropriate for the saints, and assist her in whatever she may need from you. She has been a benefactor of many people and of myself as well. (16:1–2)

These few lines will not seem like much; they may reek of polite church chatter. Yet Paul reveals here quite a lot about Phoebe. She is "our sister"—that is, she is a follower of Jesus Christ. She is from the congregation at Cenchreae, the port city of Corinth, which presumably places both her and Paul in the vicinity of Corinth for the writing of this letter.[15]

14. Although the Acts of the Apostles assumes that there can be only twelve apostles (which excludes Paul himself), Paul does not seem to think of the number as fixed (although see 1 Cor. 15:5). For a thorough discussion of the evidence about Junia, see Eldon Epp, *Junia: The First Woman Apostle* (Minneapolis: Fortress, 2005).

15. The fact that Phoebe is from Cenchreae may suggest that she is a gentile, since the Corinthian congregation seems to consist largely if not entirely of gentile believers. No evidence has been found in Cenchreae for Jewish settlement in this period (i.e., no synagogue remains, no identifiably Jewish artifacts); see Robert Jewett, *Romans: A Commentary*, Hermeneia (Minneapolis: Fortress, 2007), 945.

Paul uses two important terms for Phoebe, *diakonos* (deacon) and *prostatis* (benefactor). When I pick up a new translation of the Bible or a new commentary on Romans, this is one of the passages I check first, because that Greek word *diakonos* has been rendered with a range of English nouns—from "deacon" to "minister" to "servant" to "deaconess." To be sure, in the various small and emerging congregations of the first century, a *diakonos* is not someone who enters into a period of training and after that carries out specific roles in the life of the church. Yet it seems clear that, for Paul, the term must connote something of significance, since he applies it both to Jesus Christ (Rom. 15:8) and to himself (1 Cor. 3:5; 2 Cor. 3:6). When Paul says that Phoebe is a *deacon*, then, he probably does not mean just that she helps out in the kitchen (or that she is a "dear Christian woman," as in the Living Bible). Some quality of leadership is connoted by the term.

That hunch is reinforced by the second word, *prostatis*, which again has been translated in a variety of ways (assistant, helper, servant), the most appropriate of which is "patron," or better, "benefactor." There is considerable evidence for the importance of the patronage system in the Roman world, in which individuals who were further up the food chain made gifts to those further down, in exchange for honor and loyalty. And women were among the patrons, whether to individuals (gifts or loans or favors from one woman to another) or to groups or even cities (meals distributed to children throughout a city).[16] Although we assume that women in the Roman world were excluded from public life, law and practice did not always coincide. The satirist Juvenal (the first century's Stephen Colbert, but with more acid and less charm) opines that the best path

16. Carolyn Osiek and Margaret Y. MacDonald, *A Woman's Place: House Churches in Earliest Christianity* (Minneapolis: Fortress, 2006), 194–219.

to social advancement is through the favors of a wealthy, old woman (*Sat.* 1.39). Juvenal also complains that women not only host dinner parties but even have the audacity to talk about literature, philosophy, and politics. Presumably Juvenal would not have been at all amused by Phoebe. As a *prostatis*, a patron, she would have advanced Christian mission in some concrete ways. In short, if first-century churches had buildings and the buildings had wall plaques, Phoebe's name might well appear at the top of the list. (This means that paraphrasing "benefactor" with "she has been helpful," as the New Living Translation does, considerably understates Paul's identification of her and her importance.)

Paul goes on to say that Phoebe "has been a benefactor *of many people and of myself as well.*" Paul's work with his own hands was not enough to supply the needs of his mission, as we see here and elsewhere. Phoebe's support may include hosting Christian gatherings in her home, but that is not to identify her as an early Christian Martha Stewart, the sleek hostess offering her designer kitchen for the weekly potluck supper. The home was itself a much more public place than is typically the case in the contemporary West, and householders received business associates or clients in their homes, not in spaces dedicated as offices. To say that women taught at home or convened groups at home is not to segregate, as this is where the action was. Where else would they be?

It is likely, then, that Phoebe is a person of some means. I deduce that point not simply from the identification of her as a "deacon" and a "benefactor" but also from the fact that she has the ability to travel to Rome. Apparently she has her own funds, since if she were married and making use of her husband's money, Paul would probably have referred to her husband. (That would have been the custom.) At least *some* of the earliest Christians were people of standing and means who put their resources and prestige at the disposal of the mission.

This is a considerable introduction, but why does it appear? Probably it appears because Phoebe is the bearer of the letter, as most interpreters agree. The only reliable mail service that existed was used entirely for the official business of government. Private letter writers who were wealthy used slaves; others did the best they could, generally seeking a friend or acquaintance traveling to the destination of the letter.[17] It seems clear that Paul commends Phoebe because she carries the letter.

That point is worth enjoying for a moment. Paul writes these lines by way of introducing her to the gathered faithful in Rome. She has come to Rome and has brought the letter with her. This letter—the one that stands first in the Pauline canon, the one over which an ocean of ink has been spilled, over which countless theological battles have been waged (and are still being waged), on the perilous rocks of which exegetical careers have been made and lost—this letter was delivered by a woman. There is an irony in that detail that is perhaps best appreciated when you consider that the history of Pauline interpretation (to our knowledge) has been an overwhelmingly male endeavor.

Let's tease out this point a bit further. If Phoebe is the carrier of the letter, and most scholars agree on that point, then she was almost certainly engaged in discussing its content in advance. Paul did not simply identify someone he happened to know in Cenchreae, or someone who was already headed to Rome on a quick business trip, and then ask her to take along the letter. That much is clear from what he says about Phoebe. Given the importance Paul attaches to this letter, how likely is it that he would entrust it to someone who does not know rather

17. Klauck, *Ancient Letters*, 60–66.

specifically what he wants the letter to achieve? He would not have entrusted the letter to Phoebe without making sure that she understood its content and could represent it.

Phoebe may even have had a hand in shaping the content of the letter. That may seem an outlandish suggestion. The problem is that we tend to think of Paul's authorship of letters as a solitary act. We talk as if Paul sat at his desk the way I sit at mine and wrote as an isolated individual who had a particular set of ideas he wanted to express. Already the analogy suggests problems with this "Lone Ranger" notion. None of us writes alone. Even when we are frantically writing at 3:00 a.m., and ours is the only window on the street where the light still shines, we are writing with others. The others may be the colleagues who will read through the report, or the professor whose goodwill we hope to earn (to say nothing of a good grade), or the parishioners who chat over coffee. No one writes alone.

In Paul's world especially, writing was not done alone. Writers did not stake out a carrel in the library or even a corner table at Starbucks. While he was in Corinth, Paul was a guest in the home of Gaius (Rom. 16:23), and he very likely dictated his letter to Tertius (see 16:22) in the midst of the busy comings and goings that made the "private" realm far more public than most contemporary Westerners can imagine.

Even if Paul somehow "composed" or dictated in private, it is quite likely that some or all of this letter was read aloud to Gaius's household and guests, whose responses shaped the letter in the form in which it arrived in Rome. This much we can be fairly sure about, given what we know about the way both teaching and writing were done in the ancient world. Phoebe in particular, as the carrier of the letter, may have been involved in responding to early drafts and shaping the direction of the final letter. This suggestion takes us rather deeply into the land

13

of speculation, but at the very least, Paul would have discussed the letter with her prior to her departure for Rome.

There is yet another point to make, which is that Phoebe is also the one who reads the letter at Rome. After all, she is the one Paul commends. Perhaps others travel with her, but it is Phoebe whom Paul commends to the faithful, so surely it is Phoebe who best represents his argument.[18]

Further, if Phoebe does read the letter, then she is the first interpreter of the letter. That may seem a stretch, but it is actually pretty obvious. To read is to interpret. We experience that with the daily news—the headlines of the day sound one way on MSNBC, another on PBS, and yet another on Fox News. We all experience the power of readings in every service of public worship. Whether the Scripture lessons accuse us, comfort us, or simply bounce off unattended has a great deal to do with how they are read.

Almost inevitably, Phoebe shaped the hearing of the letter by the way she read it, whether she rushed through some passages, lingered over others, paused to allow the words to sink in, or stopped to add an explanatory note at various points. Phoebe had a role in interpreting the letter. She and Paul may even have talked about what sort of delivery he wanted, but when the time came and especially as questions arose, she was on her own.

Even if she did not read the letter herself, she would have been responsible for seeing that it circulated among the congregations at Rome, where her comments about it and her conversation with others after their hearing of the letter would have played a role in its reception.

18. This is a disputed point, as some assume Phoebe would not have been capable of reading the letter. To be sure, literacy rates were low, and the literacy rate of women was even lower than that of men. Nevertheless, some women did read, and those who did were located precisely among the women of resources such as Phoebe. See William Harris, *Ancient Literacy* (Cambridge, MA: Harvard University Press, 1989), especially 48, 67, 96, 103, 108, 140, 173, 252–63, 271, 328.

Paul and His Purposes in Romans

This exploration of the persons involved in composing, delivering, and hearing Paul's Letter to the Romans may help to render it less abstract and remote, but we have not yet touched on the question of why Romans looks the way it does. Why did Paul write this particular letter?

Answering that question for Paul's other letters is a bit easier. Beneath the effusive thanksgivings of 1 Thessalonians 1 and 2, it is not difficult to see Paul's concern for the community's persistence in the gospel (see 1 Thess. 3:1–10) and especially for the community's behavior (see 1 Thess. 4:1–12). Galatians makes it obvious early on that Paul regards the activity of some other Jewish Christian missionaries to be so wrongheaded that he calls it "another gospel," which does not even exist (1:6–9). Scholars disagree about the specifics of these situations, but the clues they work with lie ready to hand.

Romans offers few such clues about the hopes and concerns that prompt the letter and shape its content. In the opening lines of Romans 1 and in the closing discussion in Romans 15, Paul comments in general terms about his work and his planned trip to Rome (as well as to Jerusalem and Spain), but the body of the letter frustrates our detective work with its silence. Why does he write at such length about human sin, for example, when his other letters have far less to say on that topic? And what prompts the need to discuss God's relationship with Israel at such length and in such a meandering fashion (chaps. 9–11)?

One possibility is that, although the other letters address specific problems or concerns, Romans is more of an essay, perhaps even Paul's theological magnum opus. Earlier generations thought of Romans as just such an essay, and this seems a reasonable suggestion until we consider the context in which Paul worked. He was not an intellectual with leisure time for reflection and writing on the state of the world. Given what we learn of him from his other letters, supplemented by the Acts of the Apostles, Paul was intensely and constantly engaged in introducing the gospel in cities across the Mediterranean world. He worked to support himself, which gave him opportunities for talking with people about the gospel while avoiding the charge of hucksterism. That makes it a bit difficult to imagine his having the leisure for contemplating his "big" reflective essay. Scholars largely agree that this letter, like Paul's other letters, addresses some particular concern.

Having that agreement does not yield agreement about the situation itself. In fact, the problem is so widely discussed by scholars that it carries its own title: "the Romans debate."[19] The proposals are many and varied, and here I will provide only a few possibilities to give the flavor of the discussion.[20] One helpful way to think of the debate is by way of Romans 15:22–29, where Paul announces, "I am going to Jerusalem," after which he plans to travel to Rome and then to Spain. Each of these locations serves as the focal point for suggestions about the letter's purpose.

First, Jerusalem. Paul is about to leave for Jerusalem, delivering to Christians there the funds collected from his gentile churches in Macedonia and Achaia.[21] His anxious plea for prayers on behalf of this mission (15:30–32) reveals his worry that the fund might be refused, presumably because accepting

19. Karl P. Donfried edited a collection of essays on the problem in 1977 with the title *The Romans Debate* (Minneapolis: Augsburg). The book was revised and expanded in 1991 (Peabody, MA: Hendrickson) and was reissued in 2011 (Grand Rapids: Baker Academic). It still provides a helpful sampling of major views.

20. In addition to and updating Donfried's collection, see the survey in A. Andrew Das, *Solving the Romans Debate* (Minneapolis: Fortress, 2007), 9–52.

21. Paul writes about the collection(s) in Gal. 2:10; 1 Cor. 16:1–4; and especially 2 Cor. 8–9. For an extensive study, see David J. Downs, *The Offering of the Gentiles: Paul's Collection for Jerusalem in Its Chronological, Cultural, and Cultic Contexts* (Grand Rapids: Eerdmans, 2016).

the money means acknowledging Paul's understanding of the gospel, which includes his notion that Christ is for all people, gentiles included. And that inclusion does not require gentiles to be circumcised or follow Torah. For those who emphasize Jerusalem, Romans is something like Paul's rehearsal of what he will say in Jerusalem, by way of urging Roman Christians to pray for him.

Second, Spain. As Paul also indicates, he intends to go from Rome to Spain. For that he needs support, and some think Paul writes Romans in order to lay the groundwork for seeking support—material and otherwise—for that new venture. He does seem to hint at this in 15:24, when he comments that he hopes to be "sent on" to Spain by the Romans. In addition, his request that the Romans provide Phoebe with whatever she might need (16:2) could be connected with his plans for the Spanish mission.

Third, Rome. Most proposals focus the reasons for Paul's letter on Rome itself. One popular argument is that Paul is aware of conflict at Rome between Jewish and gentile believers (drawing especially on Rom. 14). Another is that Paul is aware that the Jewish Christian missionaries who proved so problematic to him in the Galatian congregations are making their way to Rome, where they will again insist (or have already insisted?) that gentiles abide by Jewish law. Yet another suggestion is that Paul fears that word of the conflict in the Galatian churches has preceded him to Rome, where he is understood to be an antinomian who has abandoned Jewish tradition.

These are not all mutually exclusive options. Paul certainly hopes for support for the Spanish mission (although it is not at all clear that this desire proves a major factor in the content of the letter). His anxiety about Jerusalem and the reception of his understanding of the gospel there also seems clear, given his repeated emphasis on God's welcome of both Jew and gentile.

Yet more may be involved here than an affirmation of God's persistent faithfulness to Israel and radical welcome of gentiles. While not in any way undermining that faithfulness, Paul locates God's faithfulness and God's radical welcome *within* a larger context, which involves the whole of the created order. The letter demonstrates this vastness, which means that, in a sense, Romans is a proclamation of the gospel, just as Paul himself says in 1:15.[22] He fears that the Romans have not heard the gospel in its fullness.

Most readers of Romans have no need to declare their allegiance for one or another of the proposals from among this dizzying array. Indeed, it may be a mistake to tie our readings too tightly to any particular view, as there may well be more than one angle in play. The benefit of keeping these various possibilities in mind is that they may help us to think of this as a real letter, rather than (again) treating it as a reflective essay on abstract issues that have little traction in real life.

A Few Words about Being "in" Romans

Before we turn to the letter itself, a few words about reading Romans may be helpful. Anyone who picks up this book already knows the dangers of proof-texting. We experience the problem routinely when the single comment of any individual metastasizes into a public nightmare via Twitter or Facebook. Wrenching comments out of context has become a way of life in our public discourse, to the detriment of the common good. Well before the rise of the Twitterverse, however, the

---

22. This also accounts for Paul's statement in 15:20 that he does not preach "where Christ is already named." It may be that he thinks Christ is not in fact fully "named" in Rome. See Beverly Roberts Gaventa, "'To Preach the Gospel': Romans 1,15 and the Purposes of Romans," in *The Letter to the Romans*, ed. Udo Schnelle, BETL 226 (Leuven: Peeters, 2009), 179–95.

difficulties involved in proof-texting from the Bible were already painfully obvious, as when Jesus's statement that "you always have the poor with you" (Mark 14:7; Matt. 26:11; John 12:8 NRSV) provided an excuse for neglecting the needs of others, to say nothing of actually supporting corrupt social systems.

Strangely enough, despite the fact that we know these dangers elsewhere, we often still read Romans as if it were a collection of isolated statements that can be plucked from context and spun out into independent sermonettes. Perhaps the most obvious example is that of Romans 8:28: "We know that all things work together for good for those who love God" (NRSV).[23] Beginning with this verse, greeting cards, tea towels, and devotional literature promote the notion that those who love God sufficiently can find good in anything, no matter how abysmal the circumstance. The moral offered, implicitly or explicitly, is that we need to be sure we love God "enough" to be able to discern the hidden nugget of goodness in whatever life puts on the table. Yet this statement sits squarely between comments about the work of the Spirit as intercessor and that of God, who calls and sets "us" apart as brothers and sisters of the firstborn, far removed from moralism.

Even those who recognize such egregious examples can still find themselves treating this letter as if it were a collection of steps on an escalator, each of which has exactly the same importance as every other step. But Romans is not a collection of individual propositions or maxims, each of which bears the same weight as every other. It is far more intricate and requires us to read carefully for context, for transitions, even for twists and turns that displace or reinterpret previous statements.

23. As the notes in the NRSV indicate, there are some differences among ancient manuscripts at this point, and there are translation questions, but these have no bearing on my point at present.

For example, in the second half of Romans 2, Paul addresses those who call themselves Jews.[24] First he asks whether those same people who identify themselves as Jews break the law, and then he undermines the categories of Jew and gentile by arguing that uncircumcised people who keep the law have priority over Jews who do not. By the time the chapter ends, it seems obvious that being a Jew has no real benefit attached to it, which is exactly the conclusion dangled at the beginning of chapter 3. Yet, having introduced that possibility, Paul immediately insists that the benefit of being a Jew is "much in every way."[25] Part of the challenge of reading Romans is to be alert for such twists and turns, rather than isolating individual statements.

Even in the case of what are obviously important moments in the letter, we need to read both forward and backward. Most interpreters of Paul agree that in 1:16–17 we have an important declaration, something like a "thesis" for the whole letter:

> For I am not ashamed of the gospel, for it is God's own power bringing about salvation for everyone who believes, the Jew first and also the Greek. For in the gospel God's rectification is being apocalyptically revealed from faith for faith, just as it is written, "The righteous one will live from faith."

As readers, we could spend a very long time unpacking the implications of these verses. What does Paul mean by salvation? by rectification (righteousness)?[26] by faith? We only have a clue

24. Whether they actually are Jews or gentiles who affiliate with Jews is a disputed matter we can set aside for now.

25. The questions of 3:1 may well reflect Paul's use of a rhetorical device, with which he introduces views opposed to his own in order to correct them. Yet that device does not undermine my point, since whoever voices Jewish advantage in 3:2, that assertion would still come as a surprise to an audience that had just heard Rom. 2.

26. Translating *dikaiosynē* and words related to it is extremely difficult, and not only because it is always challenging to take terms across language borders. Different translations reflect both long-standing debates about Pauline theology and contemporary disputes about the contexts of his letters. When I identify "righteousness" as

about what Paul is getting at when we have read the remainder of the letter. We cannot interpret this thesis statement at the outset or apart from the whole of the letter.

In the chapters that follow, we will see more of the intricacy that is Romans. For now what matters is understanding that Romans has surprises for its careful readers. And some of those surprises may even be offensive. Despite the innocuous way in which Paul's letters are often read and interpreted, they are far from innocuous. They usher us into a gospel far more vast than we usually imagine, and that gospel may well take us places we would prefer not to go.[27]

"rectification" or "God's way of making things right," I am signaling that I regard "righteousness" to be, in Paul's view, more than a quality of God; it is God's active, powerful intervention to redeem the whole of the cosmos. See especially J. Louis Martyn, "God's Way of Making Right What Is Wrong," in *Theological Issues in the Letters of Paul* (Nashville: Abingdon, 1997), 141–56.

27. Notice John 21:18.

1

WHEN IN ROMANS . . .
WATCH THE HORIZON

On a Saturday afternoon, I was waiting in the lobby before a matinee at the local movie theater. I no longer remember what film I saw, as the little drama that unfolded in the lobby more than eclipsed my memory of the one for which I had paid admission. Two people exited another of the small theaters and instigated an argument with the teenager who had been left in charge for the afternoon. They were demanding to have their admission fee returned because they hated the movie and therefore did not think that they should have to pay for it. After all, they reported, they had watched only the first ten minutes before deciding to leave. The hapless teenager could not find a way to persuade them that only the manager, who was not in the building, possessed such authority.

On the next Saturday afternoon, I was of course drawn back to watch the offending film, which was Terrence Malick's *The*

Tree of Life. I do not know whether there were more confrontations that afternoon between annoyed patrons and staff members, but I do know that not everyone loved the movie. Periodically throughout the course of the showing, someone would simply rise and walk out of the theater.

Something about the movie gives offense, but that offense has nothing to do with the usual provocations. There is no explicit sexual encounter. There is little violence. There is no overt ideological leaning that would scandalize one group or another. My evidence is entirely anecdotal, but it seems that the scandal of *The Tree of Life* has to do with the fact that it is not linear. We expect movies to have a story: there is a beginning, a middle, and an end. Flashbacks and flash forwards (more technically: analepses and prolepses) can enhance a film, but only if eventually we can track how they are incorporated into the story line.

With *The Tree of Life*, however, the narrative itself threatens to disappear. There is a story line, of sorts, about the love and loss of a single small family living in Waco, Texas, in the 1950s. Yet the heart of this film is found less in that nuclear family than in the relationship between these people and creation, or better, between them and the creator. We see miniatures of family life—playing outside, working in the kitchen garden, learning to catch a ball—and we watch as those miniatures transform into brilliant, even stunning, depictions of creation. The delights of the ordinary and the magnificence of all creation are juxtaposed with one another.[1]

For me, *The Tree of Life* was far from offensive. I experienced it as an extended doxology as it narrates the joys and trials of one family within the larger story of the creation and

---

1. Those who are familiar with Malick's work will recognize that much of what I write here about *The Tree of Life* obtains for his other films as well. I am indebted to Matthew Gaventa for instructive conversation about Malick's style.

its creator.[2] By "doxology" I do not mean an unreflective singing of "Praise God from whom all blessings flow." Sometimes the singing of the doxology is the liturgical equivalent of the seventh-inning stretch, the difference being that we bring more enthusiasm to "Take Me Out to the Ball Game." And by "doxology" I certainly do not refer to the tepid praise music that sometimes passes for doxology, in which the focus is all on "our"—or even "my"—love for Jesus or how "my" God is better than that of my neighbor's. What I have in mind is the doxology reflected in Handel's "Hallelujah Chorus" or the Widor Toccata, vast sound that crashes over us and unsettles us with its sheer majesty.

Especially when it comes to thinking about Paul's understanding of salvation, the Letter to the Romans is a little like Malick's *The Tree of Life*. Paul too locates human life in an almost unimaginably large context. The difficulty is that most of us miss those transformations. We miss the sheer size of the letter, because we have learned to notice only certain moments in the letter. It isn't that the letter has offended us; we don't walk out and demand our money back. Yet we are missing a large part of the story, and the part we are missing is crucial. It's as if we were using some odd, distorting lenses: instead of 3-D, we are using 1-D lenses that produce a flattened-out Romans, in which only a very limited story is being told.

I suspect that most of us are quite comfortable with our nice, small, domesticated version of Romans, the one that has a well-defined beginning, middle, and end. For years now I have taught courses on Romans. As a way of finding out what

2. Several people with whom I have spoken about *The Tree of Life* have seen theodicy as a central issue in the film, and it is undeniable that central characters struggle with that question. In my view, however, the film's response to questions of theodicy is the juxtaposition of the micro with the macro. And it is that very juxtaposition I find suggestive for reconsidering Romans.

understandings students bring to the subject, I often begin the course by asking them to tell me how they would describe the letter to someone who has never read it. One regular response is that the letter is about "sin, salvation, and sanctification," divided up into chapters 1–4 (sin), chapters 5–11 (salvation), and chapters 12–16 (sanctification).[3] Later on, I will have a lot to say about the limitations of that view, but at the moment I am more concerned with the breeziness of it. At least sometimes when I hear that phrase, "sin, salvation, and sanctification," or "justification by grace through faith," or even "the righteousness of God," I wonder whether it reflects a genuine struggle to read and understand the text.

Perhaps I am being unfair, since my question falls at the very beginning of a semester-long course, and students can respond only briefly in class. Yet I confess I am sometimes more encouraged by students whose response is, "I don't know even how to think about that question," than by those who immediately lay out trim slogans that barely skim the surface. So much of Christian encounter with Scripture in general consists of skimming the surface, looking for easy answers or slogans, settling for something that can be controlled or manipulated for our own ends.[4] What such readings seem to need is a text that will not hurt anyone, will not challenge or correct or enlarge.[5] Careful reading of Scripture, however, will mean, in the words

3. I am uncertain whether this schema places the treatment of God and Israel in chaps. 9–11 with 1–8 or with 12–16. The difficulty with assigning 9–11 to either category is only one of the many problems with this way of reading the letter.

4. Mary Gordon captures this tendency when she writes: "All Christians read like editors, holding in our hands a pencil that we do not fear to use whenever we see fit. Perhaps it is more true to say: all Christians are bowdlerizers. When we come to something we cannot or will not accept, we skip over it, hoping to find something we are happy to hold on to in the next chapter" (*Reading Jesus* [New York: Pantheon, 2009], xvi–xvii).

5. As a student at Union Theological Seminary (NYC) in the early 1970s, I heard James A. Sanders remark, "If you read the Bible and it makes you feel warm and cozy inside, you may be sure that you are reading it wrong." There is a place for readings

of Karl Barth, "much sweat and many groans."[6] And when it comes to the question of salvation in particular, a prolonged and careful study of Romans means finding that salvation is far more complex, more cosmic,[7] more challenging than we have usually imagined.

Although I may quibble with my students' slogans, I agree when they identify salvation as central to Romans. But what does Paul mean by salvation? The answer to that question may be larger than we have understood.

Salvation in Romans: Conventional Assumptions

When we think about salvation in Paul's Letter to the Romans, two texts come to mind immediately. The first is from what is widely regarded as the thesis of the entire letter:

> I am not ashamed of the gospel, for it is God's own power bringing about salvation for everyone who believes, the Jew first and also the Greek. (1:16)

The second text occurs within Paul's extended discussion of God's dealings with Israel:

> If you confess with your mouth that Jesus is Lord and you believe in your heart that God raised him from the dead, you will be saved. (10:9)

---

that comfort, of course, especially comfort for the grieving, the marginalized, and the afflicted. There is, nonetheless, wisdom in Sanders's comment.

6. Karl Barth, *The Epistle to the Romans*, trans. Edwyn C. Hoskyns (Oxford: Oxford University Press, 1933), 17.

7. In this context, the term "cosmic" has to do with everything that exists: human beings, animals and plant life, and larger-than-human beings as well. What it tries to capture is Paul's comprehensive understanding of the gospel. See Beverly Roberts Gaventa, "Neither Height nor Depth: Discerning the Cosmology of Romans," *SJT* 64 (2011): 265–78.

Others may come to mind as well, especially 13:11 ("Salvation is nearer than when we began to believe"). Relying on these texts and influenced by a large dose of American individualism, it is easy to think of salvation as a transaction between God and humanity, perhaps even between God and an individual. God sends Jesus as a kind of "offer" made to humanity, in response to its sins. Those who repent and believe in Jesus are saved, and those who do not repent and believe are not saved. Each individual human is confronted with this opportunity to be saved.[8]

A number of scholarly treatments of Romans presuppose this understanding. Douglas Moo, for example, identifies salvation as "spiritual deliverance," which includes restoring the sinner to a share of God's own glory.[9] Joseph Fitzmyer comments that salvation involves the whole person,[10] presumably meaning each individual person. Concerned with articulating the eschatological character of salvation, Ben Witherington and Darlene Hyatt insist that "one is not eternally secure until one is securely in eternity,"[11] again suggesting that salvation pertains to the individual human being. (Ironically, just as I wrote that sentence, an email blast arrived announcing a seminar on retirement with the words, "I promise to make you feel secure, today, tomorrow and in the future." On some interpretations of the New Testament, the gospel of God's salvation is understood to be interchangeable with and equivalent to a healthy retirement fund.)

8. In his *The Deliverance of God: An Apocalyptic Rereading of Justification in Paul* (Grand Rapids: Eerdmans, 2009), Douglas Campbell argues fiercely against this reading of Paul. While I agree with many of his conclusions, I have some serious reservations about the route he takes to get there; see my review in *Christian Century*, May 18, 2010, 35–36.
9. Douglas J. Moo, *The Epistle to the Romans*, NICNT (Grand Rapids: Eerdmans, 1996), 66–67.
10. Joseph A. Fitzmyer, *Romans*, AB 33, ed. William Foxwell Albright and David Noel Freedman (New York: Doubleday, 1993), 592.
11. Ben Witherington III and Darlene Hyatt, *Paul's Letter to the Romans: A Socio-Rhetorical Commentary* (Grand Rapids: Eerdmans, 2004), 51.

In all these instances and many others that could be cited, the assumption is that salvation has primarily to do with the individual human being, who is forgiven, restored to right relationship with God, and thereby saved from eschatological wrath and for the Christian life (hence the slogan of "sin, salvation, and sanctification").

Corporate Understandings of Salvation

In the past several decades in Pauline studies, this controlling assumption about individual salvation has come under sharp criticism for being entrenched in Western, especially American, individualism. Swimming in the cultural soup of Western education, technology, and economy, and especially in the last century of psychology, we invariably read Paul's letters (along with other ancient texts) as concerned with individuals. What we fail to understand is that the ancient world was far more collective in its thinking, filtering the world through the needs of the group rather than the individual. As a result of this important criticism, scholars have argued that Paul's letters concern people groups rather than individuals.[12]

Alternatives to these individualistic readings of Romans have emerged in several different, even conflicting forms. One approach argues that Paul's letter is concerned entirely with Christian gentiles as a people, a group.[13] Pamela Eisenbaum

12. Critiques of the overemphasis on the collective instead of the individual are emerging; see Gary W. Burnett, *Paul and the Salvation of the Individual*, BibInt 57 (Leiden: Brill, 2001). Burnett notes that the increasing use of social-scientific theory in biblical studies may play a role in this overemphasis on the group or collective, since social scientists "have a vested interest in pointing to the ways in which the individual is formed by groups and identifies with groups" (10). See also Ben C. Dunson, *Individual and Community in Paul's Letter to the Romans*, WUNT 2.232 (Tübingen: Mohr Siebeck, 2012).

13. The term "Christian" is admittedly anachronistic; it came into use only after Paul's letters were written. To make matters worse, it reinforces the notion that already

is among those who contend that in Romans the gospel, the good news, is entirely addressed to the gentiles. In Paul's view, Jews already are in covenant with God on the basis of divine grace; Jews are already justified. Paul's gospel about Jesus Christ is that "God has now extended grace to Gentiles."[14] It is gentiles as a people who stand in need of the gospel, rather than Jews.

In N. T. Wright's view, by contrast, salvation concerns the very Jewish notion of delivering Israel as a people from oppression, specifically oppression by Rome.[15] By virtue of its disobedience, Israel has not lived up to its vocation of dealing with the problem of sin in the world. As Israel's Messiah, Jesus takes on this role and thereby fulfills Israel's vocation and inaugurates the time of gentile inclusion in Israel.[16]

Yet another alternative to the individualistic reading of salvation figures prominently in recent discussions of Romans (and of Paul in general) and the Roman Empire. Robert Jewett is among those who contend that Paul's assertions about God's salvation are to be contrasted with that on offer by the empire. "Salvation must not be present in the accoutrements of Roman rule that filled the city to which this letter was addressed." Instead, Romans insists "that salvation exists in the seemingly powerless communities of faith established by the gospel."[17]

---

in Paul's time those who regarded Jesus as the Messiah of God had formed a religion separate from Judaism. For these reasons, scholars have tried other terms such as "believers," "saints," and "Christ-followers." Each of these alternatives presents its problems, however, and I have chosen to employ the traditional word "Christian" below, although recognizing its limitations.

14. Pamela Eisenbaum, *Paul Was Not a Christian: The Original Message of a Misunderstood Apostle* (New York: HarperCollins, 2009), 247.

15. N. T. Wright, "The Letter to the Romans," *NIB*, ed. Leander E. Keck (Nashville: Abingdon, 2002), 10:424.

16. Ibid., 401–2.

17. Robert Jewett, *Romans: A Commentary*, Hermeneia (Minneapolis: Fortress, 2007), 139.

These differing views of Romans share the conviction that salvation is to be viewed in terms that are corporate or social rather than personal or individual.

The Cosmic Horizon of Salvation

Whether we use the more traditional individual readings of Romans or the more recent corporate readings, all these views (however distinctive each may be) produce a linear story of problem and solution. There is a problem for humanity, and God addresses it. Whether the problem is for individuals or for the community as a whole, it is nonetheless a problem that is solved by God's intervention. Or at least God makes an offer about repairing it, an offer that human beings may freely either accept or decline. This way of thinking about salvation has counterparts in many forms of American religious life, and it is comparable to what we find in Peter's Pentecost sermon in Acts 2. In that account and others in Acts, Peter announces that God sent Jesus as Israel's Lord and Messiah. He then calls for repentance: "Repent, and be baptized every one of you in the name of Jesus Christ so that your sins may be forgiven; and you will receive the gift of the Holy Spirit" (2:38 NRSV).

God sees humanity's problem, sends Jesus as Messiah, and then offers humanity the possibility of repentance. We can recast the scenarios in larger terms without altering the underlying structure of the story: the offer may be made to an individual or to social groups, or it may concern political salvation. But the story line remains intact. Those who are fans of Jane Austen may see a certain commonality here, in that Austen is accused of writing the same plot in six different ways. The names of the characters change, but the story line persists.

31

All these models fall short of Paul's unsettling—cosmic—understanding of salvation. Although all of them may be incorporated into Paul's view, at least to a certain extent, all of them reduce the transaction to something small, either between God and a single human being or between God and a specific group of human beings. (Again, we have a text that requires 3-D lenses, but ours are 1-D.)

And, at least at first blush, the letter seems to be just that straightforward. Paul announces in the opening lines of the letter that the gospel has to do with salvation. It is God's power bringing about salvation, as he writes in Romans 1:16, and "power" is a word we will want to consider more closely later on. In the next section of the letter (1:18–3:20), he takes us on a fairly long tour of the problem in order to explain exactly *why* it is that humanity requires salvation. First, he draws on some conventional Jewish arguments about gentiles to write that human beings rebelled against God by refusing to acknowledge God.[18] He then (in chap. 2) takes up the categories of Jew and gentile in a tricky move that serves to destabilize them. There may be gentiles who observe the law even if they have never received it, and there may be Jews who do not observe the law they have received (2:12–24). This difficult chapter requires more attention than I will give it just now, but I want merely to stipulate that Paul is undermining these powerful identifying markers in an attempt to show that all people are in the same boat. He is not criticizing Judaism per se, but he is asserting that even the significant privileges of being a Jew, a member of God's household, do not separate Jews from wrongdoing. The argument

18. Putting it this way can be misleading, as if stereotyping went only in one direction. Gentiles had a number of stereotypes about Jews as well, as is ably documented in Menahem Stern, *Greek and Latin Authors on Jews and Judaism: Edited, with Introductions, Translations, and Commentary*, 3 vols. (Jerusalem: Israel Academy of Sciences and Humanities, 1974–84).

appears to wander, but it drives finally to 3:9: "All, both Jews and Greeks, are under the power of Sin." The collection of Scripture texts in 3:10–18 reinforces this point with its relentless refrain: "There is no one who is righteous. . . . There is no one who seeks God."[19] Finally, at 3:19–20, Paul restates his claim regarding the universal extent of the problem, this time in terms of the law: the law speaks in order to close every human mouth.

Following this elaborate statement of the human problem, the end of chapter 3 offers the "solution," in Christ Jesus.[20] God's rectification or righteousness, which is God's way of making things right, is brought about in the cross. God puts Jesus forward as a gift (we customarily call it grace) for all people, and the gift is received by faith.[21] In the discussion about Abraham in chapter 4, Paul shows that God has always acted through grace, even with Abraham.

There are some odd twists even here, especially in chapter 2 and at the beginning of chapter 3. If we move a little quickly and do not pause to ask a lot of questions, however, we can read Romans 1–4 as a straightforward account of a human

19. See my essay "From Toxic Speech to the Redemption of Doxology in Paul's Letter to the Romans," in *The Word Leaps the Gap: Essays on Scripture and Theology in Honor of Richard B. Hays*, ed. J. Ross Wagner, C. Kavin Rowe, and A. Katherine Grieb (Grand Rapids: Eerdmans, 2008), 392–408.

20. The fact that Paul first offers this analysis of the problem and then introduces (or reintroduces) Jesus Christ as the "solution" does not mean that he had earlier in his life, prior to his calling, thought of the world in these quite negative terms, for which he found Jesus as the "answer." Admittedly, we have no access to Paul's views before his "calling" or "conversion," apart from his own retrospective comments in Gal. 1 and Phil. 3, which are themselves profoundly influenced by his experience. Yet it seems more likely that his thinking moved from the gospel backward, from "solution" to "plight," as E. P. Sanders famously put it (*Paul and Palestinian Judaism: A Comparison of Patterns of Religion* [Minneapolis: Fortress, 1977], 442–47). Prior to Sanders, the same observation appears in Karl Barth (*Church Dogmatics* II/2 [London: T&T Clark, 1957], 92–93); see also J. Louis Martyn's comments on this point in *Galatians*, ed. William Foxwell Albright and David Noel Freedman, AB 33A (New York: Doubleday, 1997), 95n43.

21. On grace in Paul, see the important contribution of John M. G. Barclay, *Paul and the Gift* (Grand Rapids: Eerdmans, 2015).

problem, which God has solved in the death of Jesus Christ in order to save human beings from eschatological judgment.

All seems in order, then, when chapter 5 opens with the words, "Since we have been made right on the basis of faith, we have peace with God through our Lord Jesus Christ." That statement appears to signal a new stage in the argument. The discussion of human sinfulness is past, the discussion of the human problem has been treated, and Paul can now move on to describe the Christian life. And indeed, many treatments of Paul proceed in just that fashion, identifying chapter 5 as the beginning of Paul's description of the Christian life.[22]

That depiction works. At least it works for the first few verses. Before long, however, Paul has circled back and is talking again about sin, this time as a power named Sin who is partnered with Death itself.

Even before he takes up that discussion in the second half of chapter 5, even in the early lines about peace with God, Paul makes some comments that his first auditors may have found peculiar. Still depicting the "we" who have peace with God, who have been made right, Paul writes in verse 6 that "Christ died *while we were still weak*." The line continues: "at that time Christ died on behalf *of the ungodly*." Verse 8 is even more direct: "Christ died for us while we were *sinners*." And finally verse 10 says: "While *we were enemies* we were reconciled to God."

To contemporary readers, these statements may not seem offensive. They all depict life in the past, as Paul is contrasting "our" past with the present time of reconciliation and peace.

22. See, for example, C. E. B. Cranfield, *A Critical and Exegetical Commentary on the Epistle to the Romans: I*, ed. J. A. Emerton and C. E. B. Cranfield, ICC (Edinburgh: T&T Clark, 1975), 252, 255; Arland J. Hultgren, *Paul's Letter to the Romans: A Commentary* (Grand Rapids: Eerdmans, 2011), 197; Bruce J. Malina and John J. Pilch, *Social-Science Commentary on the Letters of Paul* (Minneapolis: Fortress, 2006), 239.

Yet this is strong stuff. The label "weak" is scarcely flattering to contemporary Westerners.[23] In Rome also it may well have been less than welcome. Certainly "ungodly" is not a tepid term. In a Jewish context, calling someone "ungodly" is not simply identifying the person as an agnostic or an atheist, someone who doesn't believe in God or doesn't observe religious practices; it often stands in opposition to the "righteous" (as in, e.g., Gen. 18:23, 25; Exod. 9:27; Ps. 1:6). "Ungodly" epitomizes the depiction of humanity in the second half of Romans 1 and recalls the scriptural quotations in 3:10–18. That there is "no one who fears God" is what it means to be godless. At least in the Gospels, the designation "sinners" refers to those who live on the margins of the community.[24] This also is a strong assertion, since even the marginalized "sinners" are part of the community and should for that reason both know and behave better than the "ungodly" (5:6). And to say that "we" were "enemies" of God is even stranger, as it depicts "us" as in conflict with God (5:10).[25]

23. Think of the constant advice to professionals not to behave in ways that seem weak, to say nothing of the fear that an American president will come across as "weak" or that the United States will be viewed as "weak" on the world stage. Contemporary illustrations abound. Mark Reasoner considers the use of the terms "strong" and "weak" in the Roman milieu (*The Strong and the Weak: Romans 14.1–15.13 in Context*, SNTSMS 103 [Cambridge: Cambridge University Press, 1999], 45–58). See the evidence he adduces as well as his conclusion: "The terms, as Paul uses them, fit the Roman tendency to define social hierarchies within various levels of early imperial society and differentiate positions in a hierarchy on the basis of status" (45).

24. Greg Carey, *Sinners: Jesus and His Earliest Followers* (Waco: Baylor University Press, 2009), 6–15. See also Elisabeth Schüssler Fiorenza, *In Memory of Her: A Feminist Theological Reconstruction of Christian Origins* (New York: Crossroad, 1985), 128.

25. I use scare quotes around "we" and "us" here and elsewhere for two reasons. First, I am trying to avoid a facile identification between Paul and contemporary readers. Second, and more important, I think it is sometimes quite unclear who "we" are in Paul's discourse. Is "we" limited to what would now be called the Christian community (as seems to be the case in 5:1–11, given what is said in 4:24–25), or does "we" look beyond to the entire human community (see 5:12–21)? Chapter 4 will explore this question further.

It may be easy for twenty-first-century readers to let these terms wash over them, but I suspect these are not terms that Paul's hearers would *ever have applied to themselves*, because they understood themselves to be among God's people or at least to be aligned with God's people. As the introduction explains, there is ongoing debate about whether the audience of this letter is largely gentile or whether it is divided between Jews and gentiles. The issues are complex, but on any proposal, the audience is not likely to take kindly to this depiction. Presumably, Jews in the Roman congregations came from within the synagogue and regarded Jesus as continuing or fulfilling God's promise to Israel, of which they were already a part. Gentile believers in this early period almost certainly came from the ranks of those who had already been associated with the synagogue.[26] If they were not full proselytes, they at least were associated with God's people and probably made that association with Judaism precisely because of its strong moral teaching. To hear themselves characterized as weak, ungodly sinners who had even been God's enemies would be more than a bit puzzling, possibly even offensive. It is all too easy to imagine someone objecting to Phoebe, the bearer and the reader of the letter, "Who you calling 'sinner,' lady?"

Paul also says other things in these lines, things having to do with the hope experienced by Christians as a result of God's love and especially with the gracious character of Jesus's death (about which I will comment later). It could be that I am making too much of this thread of negatives. Perhaps Paul includes them only for comparative purposes, as they make the Christian life seem that much better (the equivalent of an advertising strategy for a "new and improved product"). But

26. Peter Lampe, *From Paul to Valentinus: Christians at Rome in the First Two Centuries*, trans. Michael Steinhauser, ed. Marshall D. Johnson (Minneapolis: Fortress, 2003), 69.

in what follows in 5:12–21 there is almost nothing that could rightly be called a depiction of the Christian life. Instead, Paul returns to his comments about Sin, but this time Sin is accompanied by Death, and both appear as powers that rule human life.

One shorthand way of speaking about 5:12–21 is to say that Paul is contrasting Adam with Christ, but that is only part of the story.

Sin entered the world and through Sin came Death. Thus Death entered into all people. (5:12)

Death ruled as a king from Adam until Moses. (5:14)

Again later:

Death ruled as a king through the transgression of one person. (5:17)

Sin multiplied. (5:20)

Sin ruled as a king through Death. (5:21)

In chapter 6 Paul famously addresses the fear that an emphasis on grace may lead to moral laxity. Scholars often conclude that Paul is responding to charges that his preaching and teaching are antinomian. Yet even here Sin and Death continue to function as powerful figures:

Death no longer lords it over Christ. (6:9)

Do not let Sin rule as a king in your mortal body. (6:12)

Do not present your members [body parts] to Sin as weapons of wrong. (6:13)

Sin will not lord it over you. (6:14)

You were slaves of Sin. (6:17)

Even in chapter 7, with its notoriously famous monologue by the tortured "I," Sin and Death continue to dominate the discussion:

Sin took the commandment as a ground of operation and produced in me every desire. (7:8)

Sin, taking a ground of operation through the commandment, deceived me and killed me through the commandment. (7:11)

I am sold under the power of Sin. (7:14)

Sin lives in me. (7:17)

It is only in the beginning of chapter 8 that this strand disappears, when Paul declares that God has condemned Sin and has freed humanity from Sin and Death. To put it sharply and succinctly: throughout these three chapters, 5–7, we meet suprahuman powers by the names of Sin and Death. Taking advantage of the disobedience of Adam, Sin and Death make their way into the world and establish themselves as its rulers. They have humankind under their control, all humankind. They are so powerful that they can make use even of God's holy law (7:8, 11), even with those who (like the speaker in chap. 7) love God's law and are committed to obeying that law. Sin and Death are defeated only by God's action in Jesus Christ.[27]

27. See Paul W. Meyer, "The Worm at the Core of the Apple: Exegetical Reflections on Romans 7," in *The Word in This World: Essays in New Testament Exegesis and Theology*, ed. John T. Carroll (Louisville: Westminster John Knox, 2004), 57–77. See also my essays "God Handed Them Over" and "The Cosmic Power of Sin in Paul's Letter to the Romans," in *Our Mother Saint Paul* (Louisville: Westminster John Knox,

Thinking again about the film *The Tree of Life*, we may say that in Romans also the story line seems to veer off at a strange angle. The narrative of human plight followed by divine solution is already under way in chapters 1–4, when Paul doubles back to describe again the plight. And this is not simply repetition for the sake of emphasis. This time, when he describes the plight, he takes what was already said about sin and salvation and spins it out in larger, more complex, even cosmic terms. No longer is the story one of humanity that persists in sinning until God sends Jesus as a kind of sacrifice, which we might think to be the case up through chapter 3. That story morphs into a story of conflict and enslavement and deliverance. The agents in the story are not only God or Jesus Christ and humanity, but they include Sin and Death.

And there is more to come: chapter 8 famously turns to life in the Spirit, life that enables human beings to cry out to God as their father because they are themselves heirs along with Christ. In fact, Paul goes on to contend that all creation longs for redemption.[28] Paul writes confidently about hope and the intervention of the Spirit and the way in which God has already acted on humanity's behalf. Here we might expect to find a discussion of the eschaton, perhaps even have a glimpse of the triumphant return of Jesus such as we find in 1 Thessalonians 4 and 1 Corinthians 15. Paul takes us to the edge of that event with his assertions about the longing of all creation

2007), 113–35; "The Rhetoric of Violence and the God of Peace in Paul's Letter to the Romans," in *Paul, John, and Apocalyptic Eschatology: Studies in Honour of Martinus C. de Boer*, ed. Jan Krans, B. J. Lietaert Peerbolte, Peter-Ben Smit, and Arie W. Zwiep, NovTSup (Leiden: Brill, 2013), 61–75.

28. I understand Paul's use of the term "creation" to include not only nonhuman creation but also all of humanity. Further, Paul's use of *kosmos* alongside *pas* ("all") reinforces the emphasis on the universal scope of the letter. In Romans, we see repeated reference to the disobedience and sinfulness of "all" (3:23; 5:18; 11:32), as well as God's actions on behalf of "all" (1:5, 16) (see Gaventa, "Neither Height nor Depth," 266–69).

for redemption. But instead of taking up Jesus's triumphant return, the end of chapter 8 turns again to a conflict between God and God's enemies. "If God is for us, who is against us?" (8:31). He goes on: "Who will bring a charge against God's chosen? Will it be God who makes things right?" (8:33). And later still, "Who will condemn? Will it be Christ—who died, or rather who was raised, who also is at God's right hand, who intercedes for us? Who will separate us from Christ's love?" (8:34–35). There follows first a list of circumstances, including famine, hardship, and persecution. But Paul continues, "We are more than conquerors through the one who loved us" (8:37). And finally comes a list of the powers that produce the circumstances: Death, life, angels, rulers, and so forth (8:38–39). In all of this, Paul insists, nothing will have the power to separate "us" from God's love in Christ Jesus.

A close examination of each term is not necessary here, as my concern is for the general sense of this passage. We need to recognize this for what it is: trash talk. Paul looks at all the harmful circumstances in which human beings live, he sees behind those the work of God's own enemies, and he confidently declares that God will have the last word. He shakes his fist in the face of all these powers and says, "No power has the power like Christ's power." Rendered in the vernacular, what Paul means is: "You are going down."

This point is recapitulated briefly and succinctly in the closing of the letter. Often overlooked because we stop reading at the end of chapter 15, Romans 16 is quite important. The extended greetings reveal a lot about the congregations at Rome (as we saw above in the introduction), but following those greetings Paul issues warnings about false teaching and concludes with a promise, "The God of peace will quickly crush Satan under your feet" (16:20). He has not earlier in this letter referred to Satan, but here Satan appears as something of a shorthand reference to all the powers that oppose God and threaten God's people. God will bring them down. (The agency of God is crucial here: God does this, not human beings!)

We have traveled all too quickly over a lot of challenging terrain, but the point is this: *Paul's understanding of salvation is cosmic. Salvation concerns God's powerful action in Jesus Christ to reclaim humanity, individual and corporate, from the powers of Sin and Death.* The human situation is not simply that humans do bad things (or that some humans do bad things), or that gentiles now have the possibility of their own covenant with God, or that Israel is being delivered from oppression. The problem is that actual powers, prominent among them Sin and Death, hold humanity in their grasp. God has interceded in the death and resurrection of Jesus to break their power ("God condemned Sin in the flesh [of Jesus Christ]," Rom. 8:3), but the struggle between God and the powers continues until God's final triumph, the redemption of the whole of creation.

This understanding of salvation in Romans suggests that we also need a larger framework for understanding the death of Jesus. What is it that the cross accomplishes, or more specifically, how does the cross play a role in this cosmic battle? One traditional way of addressing that question is to see in Paul a notion of substitutionary sacrifice, in which Jesus dies in place of human beings as a sacrifice that addresses God's wrath. That view draws heavily on 3:21–26, where Paul uses language connected with sacrifice (God offers Jesus as the *hilastērion,* or "mercy seat"), blood, and dealing with "former sins."[29] It also

29. This is a notoriously challenging text; see especially Douglas Campbell, *The Rhetoric of Righteousness in Romans 3.21–26,* JSNTSup 65 (Sheffield: JSOT Press, 1992), and Charles B. Cousar's excellent study of this passage in *A Theology of the Cross: The Death of Jesus in the Pauline Letters* (Minneapolis: Fortress, 1990), 36–43.

relies on those places in which Paul writes that Jesus died "for us" (5:8; 8:31–32; 1 Thess. 5:10; see also 2 Cor. 5:21; Gal. 3:13) and that Jesus was "handed over" (Rom. 4:25; 8:32). These are important statements, but there are other strands interpreting Jesus's death as well. In 5:12–21, as we have seen, Jesus's obedience (to the point of death) is pivotal, not simply to the assuaging of God's wrath, but to the defeat of Sin and Death. In 6:9 Paul writes that "Death no longer rules over" Christ. These passages put Jesus's death in a larger landscape, in which his death is not simply obedient sacrifice (language more at home in the book of Hebrews than in Romans) but a turning point in the conflict between God and the anti-God powers. That possibility is underscored when Paul writes of Christ not being "withheld" but being "handed over" (4:25; 8:32), since this is language widely used in military contexts for the turning over of someone or something to another agent or power.[30]

A full-blown account of Paul's understanding of Jesus's death is not my aim here. As the earliest generation of Christians spoke of Jesus's death, they did so in a variety of ways, and Paul himself spoke of it in more than a single way. In the Corinthian correspondence, for example, the death of Jesus stands as an epistemological crisis in that it is the point at which humanity's distorted values are revealed as foolishness (1 Cor. 1:18 and 2 Cor. 5:17). In some other texts (Galatians especially), Jesus's death is an act of love (and see Rom. 5:8). But Paul can also speak of it as the turning point in a cosmic conflict, the event that inaugurates and promises God's final triumph over Sin and Death. Given Paul's depiction of a humanity (indeed, of all creation) enslaved to the powers of Sin and Death,

30. See my essays "God Handed Them Over," in *Our Mother Saint Paul*, 113–23, and "Interpreting the Death of Jesus Apocalyptically: Reconsidering Romans 8:32," in *Jesus and Paul Reconnected: Fresh Pathways into an Old Debate*, ed. Todd D. Still (Grand Rapids: Eerdmans, 2007), 125–45.

nothing less than the powerful death and resurrection of Jesus Christ can defeat the powers by "tricking" them into their own defeat. This picture seems to be at work in 1 Corinthians 2:8: "None of the powers of this age knew, for if they had known, they would not have crucified the Lord of glory." By crucifying Jesus Christ, the anti-God powers bring about their own defeat, since their destructive power is no match for God's resurrecting power.

Most people think of this as a joint action, in which salvation requires a "human response." I have said nothing yet about a human response, about the contingent character of God's action. But it may be useful just now to notice two words that have little or no place in Paul's vocabulary: "repentance" and "forgiveness." True, in Romans 2, Paul once declares that God's mercy is intended to lead to repentance, but that statement is part of his move to destabilize those who think themselves without need of repentance and is part of a larger argument undermining the categories of Jew and gentile. Nowhere else in the letter does he say that humanity needs to repent or has repented or even that humanity can repent. And nowhere does he talk of forgiveness. I think this peculiar silence occurs because Paul sees the human problem as larger than that of repentance and forgiveness of the individual. This is clear from the slavery language in Romans 6: slaves cannot repent their way out of slavery; neither can they be forgiven. They can only be delivered, which is the terminology Paul uses. Salvation, for Paul, doesn't consist of simply being forgiven for sins; it is being delivered from Sin's power.

Why It Matters

This is exceedingly uncomfortable territory. To begin with, many contemporary Westerners find any language of sin off-putting, in large part because it has been reduced to personal foibles and often employed in ways that are rigid and judgmental, to say nothing of being hypocritical. And Paul's understanding of Sin as a power (along with Death and other powers opposed to God) makes that discomfort worse rather than better. To say that God does battle with powers, that God exerts power, raises yet more problems.

In our time, "power" is a term that generates a lot of anxiety. We think rather quickly of its misuse, its unequal distribution, its distortion. And we should. We are rightly concerned about claims of divine power, since they can easily be distorted into claims that *we* are agents, even the custodians and dispensers, of God's power. But I suspect that the real objection to what I have said will have to do with my discussion of powers other than God: Does Paul really believe in such powers? What can be said about their origin? Their ontological standing? Their future? Perhaps most important: Why would we want to take such an argument seriously? Should we not, if this is really what Paul thought, simply continue to ignore it?

I contend that Paul's argument is important for us. Think for a moment about the enslaving effects that alcohol has in many human lives, or drugs, or gambling, or mental illness. People who have lived with or in the neighborhood of these illnesses know that simply telling someone to say no, to repent, is ineffective. The illness has an enslaving grasp on that person that can be broken only by intervention, by powerful intervention. That is emphatically not to claim that those who suffer from mental illness or from addiction have demons. I refer to these illnesses only illustratively, although I have found that the illustrations resonate powerfully.

To take another analogy: Paul's understanding of human life under the reign of anti-God powers looks quite a bit like what we know about the horror of the child soldier. In many parts of the world, children are swept from their villages or off the streets or traded by parents desperate for food or protection. They become little more than slaves—girls used for kitchen duty and sex, boys wielding weapons, both of them as bait. In many cases, they are forced to become soldiers. And not just to become child soldiers, but eventually to become the ones who capture and use others. There is no escape; in many cases, there is not even the hope of escape as family is destroyed and replaced, as unrelenting ideology takes over even their thoughts. They cannot help themselves; they cannot rescue themselves. They have nowhere to go. Their power consists only of self-destruction and the eventual destruction of others.[31]

Child soldiers can only be rescued. Redeemed. And power—loving power—must come from the outside to redeem them. What Paul is showing us is that "we" are all in some sense among those child soldiers. The powers to which "we" are enslaved may be less visible than those of the child soldier. In such a context, power is not to be rejected, especially when it is the self-giving power of redemption.

At the same time, the "power" to which Paul appeals is not power in the usual sense of power to overwhelm and destroy. This is not the "shock and awe" of human military force, although certainly Paul uses that language in 16:20 ("The God of peace will quickly crush Satan under your feet"). Notice, however, that it is the God of peace who accomplishes this act, just as it is the weakness of a suffering Messiah that breaks the universal, otherwise implacable hold of Sin and Death.

31. Roméo Dallaire, *They Fight like Soldiers, They Die like Children* (New York: Walker, 2010). A former member of the Canadian Armed Forces, Dallaire writes passionately about child soldiers, incorporating the horror experienced by professionally trained military personnel who find themselves faced with opponents who are mere children—untrained but desperate and armed with lightweight powerful weapons.

Every word I have written here could be (and often should be) qualified, and many other scholarly voices brought to bear. Rather than qualify everything, however, let me get to the point. What is so disruptive about Paul's understanding of salvation is his challenge to us to hear the gospel in its vastness. The vastness of what God has accomplished is far larger than the word "salvation" usually suggests. Of course, God's action in the gospel speaks to the lives of individuals, to what we often refer to as the "spiritual" life. And, of course, God's action reaches beyond the "spiritual" to include the redemption of our institutions, the reconciliation of ethnic groups, and the confrontation of empires of all sorts. If we think that God's power is restricted to the sphere of the "spiritual," then we have a fairly small notion of God. What we also need to hear is Paul's understanding that the gospel encompasses the cosmos, the whole of creation—all the way out and all the way down in human life.

And that is where Terrence Malick's *The Tree of Life* connects deeply with Paul. Not only do both of them break out of conventional linear expectations, one with a story and one in a letter, they both place human life in an almost unimaginably large context. The result is that, when we are in Romans, we always find ourselves watching the horizon.

2

WHEN IN ROMANS . . .

CONSIDER ABRAHAM

Because he died in an automobile accident in 1982, a few months shy of his fortieth birthday, Harry Chapin and his songwriting have long since faded from prominence. Chapin is probably best known for "Cat's in the Cradle," a poignant reflection on the ways parents reap for themselves their treatment of their children.[1] Like "Cat's in the Cradle," many of Chapin's songs concern people moving into middle age, but "Flowers Are Red" features a little boy and his desire to draw what he sees in his head. The child draws flowers in a rainbow of colors, but his teachers disapprove: "Flowers are red," they insist, and "green leaves are green." Over and over the exchange repeats between the child and his teachers. At

---

1. "Cat's in the Cradle" was written in collaboration with Sandy Chapin. For information about Harry Chapin and his work, see http://www.harrychapinmusic.com.

last the child finds himself in a classroom with a more open-minded teacher, one who encourages him to draw whatever he sees, however wild his pictures may be. But he can no longer imagine flowers in any other way than the way they have always been painted. The child has become what he has been taught.

Some of us resemble that little boy when it comes to reading Scripture: we know what the questions are in advance, which means we also know in advance what answers are possible. One of the challenges for the interpretation of biblical texts is that we are constrained by our predecessors so that we think largely in terms of the conventional questions our predecessors posed for the text. That is not at all to deride our predecessors or to dismiss the rich history of biblical interpretation. We need a broad range of conversation partners, but we also need from time to time to reflect critically on the questions we have inherited. When we do so, we may occasionally find ourselves backing up and imagining the questions—and the answers—differently.

One such set of constraints has to do with Paul's attitude toward Israel. Discussions have focused on whether Israel is "legalistic,"[2] or on the existence of a "spiritual" Israel, usually understood to be the church, or on the question of Israel's eschatological salvation.[3] These are not altogether bad questions, but they are a bit like asking whether the grieving family portrayed in Malick's *The Tree of Life* seeks counseling for its grief and what sort of counseling it should be (see chap. 1). That is also not a bad question, except that it altogether misses the film's

---

2. The term is already problematic as it suggests that readers have access to the minds of ancient Jews and can know their attitudes.

3. Another question that dominates discussion of Rom. 9–11 is whether Paul's stance is that of supersessionism, with some scholars accusing others of producing an exegesis of Romans that is consistent with supersessionism. Unfortunately, the word is often used dismissively, without any accompanying definition, so that it becomes a scare word. See Kendall Soulen's helpful discussion in "Supersessionism," in *A Dictionary of Jewish-Christian Relations*, ed. Edward Kessler and Neil Wenborn (Cambridge: Cambridge University Press, 2005), 413–44.

larger depiction of life between creation and consummation. In
the same way, conventional treatments of Romans 9–11 often
overlook the fact that the primary question Paul raises about
Israel is a question about God.

What I argue in this chapter is fairly simple, perhaps decep-
tively so. I contend that, for Paul in Romans, *Israel belongs to
God as God's creation.* Israel is always and only God's creation.
And Israel will remain God's creation, even in the eschaton.
"Israel" is not a term for the church or for some "spiritual"
gathering of Jewish and gentile believers. It is coterminous
with what we usually call "ethnic" Israel, but Paul does not
treat Israel as an ethnic entity; he instead treats Israel in terms
of creation and redemption. We construe the question too narrowly when we think of it as having to do with Israel's belief
or Israel's (dis)obedience. For Paul, the question of Israel is
overwhelmingly a question about God—about God's creation
and God's redemption.

For many interpreters of Romans in the period prior to the
Second World War, the question of God and Israel was a minor
way station in Paul's Letter to the Romans. In their International
Critical Commentary volume published in 1902, for example,
William Sanday and Arthur C. Headlam wrote that, with the
end of Romans 8, Paul has "finished his *main argument.* He
has expounded his conception of the Gospel. But there still
remains a difficulty which could not help suggesting itself to
every thoughtful reader . . . [namely, the fate of Israel]."[4] Writing in the early 1930s, C. H. Dodd argued that Romans 9–11 was
something of an aside and represents "a somewhat earlier piece
of work, incorporated here wholesale" in order to save Paul the
time and energy involved in composing a new treatment of the

---

4. William Sanday and Arthur C. Headlam, *A Critical and Exegetical Commentary on the Epistle to the Romans,* 4th ed., ICC (Edinburgh: T&T Clark, 1900), 225
(emphasis added).

subject.[5] Even as late as 1979, John A. T. Robinson described Romans 9–11 as a possible "excursus," although he conceded that Romans 9–11 is nonetheless "closely related to the themes of the first half of the letter."[6] As far back as the 1800s, however, the German scholar F. C. Baur claimed that this section of the epistle is "the centre and pith of the whole, to which everything else is only an addition,"[7] and this minority view has become a majority view in recent decades.[8] One of the rare points of agreement in the last several decades of Pauline scholarship is that chapters 9–11 are integral to the letter. These are not a mere aside, an appendix, or an afterthought. Indeed, in some quarters 9–11 has become *the* main point of the whole letter. Ben Witherington and Darlene Hyatt describe 9–11 as the "climax" of the whole argument.[9] A. Katherine Grieb describes it as "the very center" of the letter's argument.[10]

Such hyperbolic pronouncements stand at the other end of the pendulum swing from the minimizing claims of earlier generations. These pronouncements rightly insist that

5. C. H. Dodd, *The Epistle of Paul to the Romans*, MNTC (1932; repr., London: Collins, 1959), 150.

6. John A. T. Robinson, *Wrestling with Romans* (Philadelphia: Westminster, 1979), 109.

7. Ferdinand Christian Baur, *Paul, the Apostle of Jesus Christ, His Life and Works, His Epistles and Teachings: A Contribution to a Critical History of Primitive Christianity*, trans. A. Menzies and E. Zeller, 2nd ed. (London: Williams & Norgate, 1873–75), 327.

8. With good cause, Mark Reasoner claims that the recent trend in scholarship regarding chaps. 9–11 as an integral part of Paul's letter "represents a breathtaking change in the history of interpretation" ("Romans 9–11 Moves from Margin to Center, from Rejection to Salvation: Four Grids for Recent English-Language Exegesis," in *Between Gospel and Election: Explorations in the Interpretation of Romans 9–11*, ed. Florian Wilk and J. Ross Wagner, WUNT 257 [Tübingen: Mohr Siebeck, 2010], 79).

9. Ben Witherington III and Darlene Hyatt, *Paul's Letter to the Romans: A Socio-Rhetorical Commentary* (Grand Rapids: Eerdmans, 2004), 244.

10. A. Katherine Grieb, *The Story of Romans: A Narrative Defense of God's Righteousness* (Louisville: Westminster John Knox, 2002), 87.

the relationship between God and Israel is a crucial issue in this letter. Even those readers who might persist in thinking that the relationship between God and Israel is only a minor issue nonetheless have a responsibility to confront both Scripture's varied teaching about Israel and Christian habits of speech and action that have contributed to the horrors of anti-Judaism.

Not Entirely Random Preliminaries

Before we turn to specific texts in Romans, some stipulations are in order. First, for our purposes, it is important to distinguish the question of Paul's stance toward the Torah, the law of Moses, from his stance toward Israel as such. What he has to say about Israel may not depend on what he has been saying through much of Romans 1–8 about the law (and what he will say about the law in 9–11). And what he has to say about the law does not necessarily depend on what he has to say about Israel. In fact, at least some of Paul's comments about the law in Romans amount to a rather clever distraction. He cuts his argument one way and another throughout the letter, so that his audience remains somewhat off its guard. For example, Paul insists in 3:31 that he is upholding the law rather than undermining it, but his very next reference to the word insists that the promise to Abraham did not come through the law (4:13) and that the law produces wrath (4:15).

We also need to distinguish what Paul says about Israel from his interpretation of Israel's Scripture, which was, of course, Paul's Scripture, the only Scripture Paul knew. More than in any other of his letters, in Romans Paul draws on, makes use of, and enters into creative—sometimes mystifying—readings of the Scriptures of Israel.[11] But that reliance on, that deep engagement with, Scripture does not, in and of itself, necessarily convey anything about Paul's understanding of Israel. The fact that Paul writes with Israel's Scripture and thinks about the gospel with Israel's Scripture does not mean that he is either sympathetic or hostile to Israel. The Pharisees and the Essenes were deeply engaged with Scripture too, and their views of Israel were miles apart from one another.

Perhaps most important, we need to distinguish Paul's teaching about Israel from that of contemporary Christianity—distinguish, not separate. Paul is one voice in the large and diverse choir that makes up Scripture, and it is incumbent on Christians to listen to the whole choir. It is also important to distinguish Paul's teaching about Israel from the complex web of questions and problems concerning the contemporary nation of Israel. Paul may well have something to contribute to Christian reflection on responsibility in the public arena, and in particular with respect to the Middle East, but that contribution is not to be found solely in Romans 9–11. What I am getting at is that Paul could not have imagined the modern nation Israel, and thus his use of the noun "Israel" is not to be confused

11. Scholarly treatments of Paul's interpretation of Scripture proliferate; see especially Richard B. Hays, *Echoes of Scripture in the Letters of Paul* (New Haven: Yale University Press, 1989); Hays, *The Conversion of the Imagination: Paul as Interpreter of Israel's Scripture* (Grand Rapids: Eerdmans, 2005); J. Ross Wagner, *Heralds of the Good News: Paul and Isaiah in Concert in the Letter to the Romans*, NovTSup 101 (Leiden: Brill, 2002); Francis Watson, *Paul and the Hermeneutics of Faith* (London: T&T Clark, 2004); Dietrich-Alex Koch, *Die Schrift als Zeuge des Evangeliums: Untersuchungen zur Verwendung und zum Verständnis der Schrift bei Paulus*, BHT 69 (Tübingen: J. C. B. Mohr [Paul Siebeck], 1986); Christopher D. Stanley, *Paul and the Language of Scripture: Citation Technique in the Pauline Epistles and Contemporary Literature*, SNTSMS 74 (Cambridge: Cambridge University Press, 1992); Stanley, *Arguing with Scripture: The Rhetoric of Quotations in the Letters of Paul* (New York: T&T Clark, 2004). For a helpful orientation to the issues involved, see J. Ross Wagner, "Paul and Scripture," in *The Blackwell Companion to Paul*, ed. Stephen Westerholm (Oxford: Wiley-Blackwell, 2011), 154–71.

with that country. Nonetheless, the respect for God's creation (human and otherwise) that comes to expression in Romans is only one sliver of a vast biblical witness to the desire for the peace and flourishing of all God's people, which includes (to understate considerably) personal safety.

The Peculiar Story of Abraham: Romans 4

What Paul has to say about God's dealings with Israel comes to a head in chapters 9–11, but it is anticipated much earlier. At the very beginning of the letter, Paul establishes that Christ Jesus is born from the line of David (1:3) and that the gospel is for the Jew first (1:16). In Romans 2, as I suggested in the last chapter, he takes up the categories of Jew and gentile, only to destabilize them. Verses 12–16 conjure up the notion of gentiles, people who have not received the law, who nonetheless observe it, while verses 17–24 hold out the possibility that there may be Jews who have the law, even boast of the law, while not observing it. This amounts to a blurring of traditional lines, and Paul goes even further with this destabilizing in verses 25–29 when he insists that uncircumcision can become circumcision and circumcision can become uncircumcision. Under such circumstances, is there any benefit to being a Jew? The answer would seem to be "no," but Paul insists just the opposite: Jews have been entrusted with the "sayings," the "oracles" of God (3:2), and God remains faithful even when humans do not.

What exactly Paul means about God's entrusting Jews will be taken up again only in 9–11. Whatever it means, it does not exempt Jews from sinning, and 3:3–20 relentlessly insists that all are "under the power of Sin" (3:9), that the whole world is under God's judgment (3:19).

By the end of chapter 3, Paul has reminded his audience that God is God not only of Jews but also of gentiles and that God makes things right ("justifies" is how we usually translate it) for both Jews and gentiles in the same way. There is a bit of an argumentative sleight of hand here, one to which those of us who are heirs of gentile Christianity are often insensitive, if not oblivious. Of course, God must be the God of Jews as well as gentiles, since God is the creator of all. But Paul has pushed this agreed-upon claim (if there is only one God, then God must be over all) to a conclusion that not all Jews would find so agreeable: God deals with Jews and gentiles *in the same way.*[12] In chapter 4, in his discussion of Abraham, he will stretch that claim to a conclusion that could be downright offensive.

Translating Romans 4:1 is notoriously difficult. The NRSV represents a conventional view that it is Abraham who is the seeker: "What then are we to say was gained by Abraham, our ancestor according to the flesh?" Other translations similarly make Abraham the one who "found" or "gained" something (see, for example, the KJV, NIV, NRSV, and NASB). By contrast, some scholars have suggested that the question actually concerns "our" finding about Abraham: "Have we found Abraham to be our forefather according to the flesh?"[13] On either translation, the question suggests that *Abraham* is about to be the

12. Terence L. Donaldson notes that the impartiality of God is a theme found in the Old Testament and elsewhere (cf. Sir. 35:15–16; Jub. 5:16; 21:4; 30:18; 2 Bar. 44:4; T. Job 43:13). According to Donaldson, "God's impartiality is evident—negatively in that the whole world, without distinction, is held accountable for its sin (3:19); and positively in that the righteousness of God is available for all without distinction (3:22). It is at this point—not the move from impartiality to Gentile salvation per se, but the intermediate moves in which sin is used to nullify the traditional covenantal function of the law—that Paul can be said to be turning this Jewish axiom against the basic convictions of covenantal nomism" (*Paul and the Gentiles: Remapping the Apostle's Convictional World* [Minneapolis: Fortress, 1997], 93).
13. Richard B. Hays, "'Have We Found Abraham to Be Our Forefather according to the Flesh?' A Reconsideration of Romans 4:1," *NovT* 27, no. 1 (1985): 76–98; T. Zahn, *Der Brief des Paulus an die Römer* (Leipzig: Deichert, 1910), 21.

focus of the argument. That is not particularly surprising, as numerous Jewish and early Christian texts pay close attention to Abraham. What follows is strange, however, both for *what it says* about Abraham and for *what it does not say*.

Imagine, by way of analogy, that you find a new biography of another Abraham, Abraham Lincoln. You are intrigued, and you begin to read. What you find surprises you. The book repeatedly describes Lincoln as the first Republican president, the inaugurator of a line of Republican leaders running through to the present day. Yet the same book never mentions his impoverished childhood or the issuing of the Emancipation Proclamation. You would certainly suspect that the author was up to something strange. Similarly, Paul appears to be up to something in his recasting of the story of Abraham.

First, in Romans 4 Paul repeatedly discusses Abraham's faith or trust in God, but he never mentions Abraham's obedience. But the very Genesis narrative on which Paul draws underscores Abraham's obedience. Without hesitation, Abraham picks up and moves from Haran to Canaan on the Lord's command (Gen. 12:4). Again in response to God's command, Abraham undergoes circumcision and in turn circumcises the males of his household (Gen. 17). And, of course, Abraham obeys God when he prepares to sacrifice his son Isaac in response to the divine demand (Gen. 22). Not surprisingly, Abraham's obedience features prominently in Jewish texts of the Second Temple period. For example, Sirach's praise of Israel's ancestors summarizes Abraham in this way:

> Abraham was the great father of a multitude of nations, and no one has been found like him in glory. He kept the law of the Most High, and entered into a covenant with him; he certified the covenant in his flesh, and when he was tested he proved faithful. Therefore the Lord assured him with an oath that the

nations would be blessed through his offspring. (Sir. 44:19–21a NRSV; see also Wis. 10:5; 1 Macc. 2:52; 4 Macc. 16:20)

Early Christian texts make similar claims about Abraham's obedience. In the Acts of the Apostles, Stephen's comments about Abraham focus almost entirely on God's promise. Stephen attributes to Abraham but a single action, that of following God's commandment to move from Mesopotamia to Haran (7:3–4). In the book of Hebrews, Abraham is introduced with the words "By faith, Abraham obeyed . . ." (11:8). In the context of the larger tradition, according to which Abraham's faith is equated with his obedience (to the call to migrate, to the command for circumcision, to the sacrifice of Isaac), Paul's silence on this motif is surely noteworthy, like the dog that does not bark.

Not only is Paul silent about Abraham's obedience, but he also insistently connects Abraham with uncircumcised gentiles rather than identifying him as the biological father of Israel (as Rom. 4:1 might suggest).[14] Romans 4:9 begins this association by introducing the seemingly naive question about God's blessing "apart from works" (4:6): Does God's blessing fall on the circumcised or on the uncircumcised? In the narrow context of the citation from Psalm 32:1–2 (31:1–2 LXX) that precedes, this appears to be a general question, but verses 9b and 10 make clear that the question is about Abraham: Was he circumcised or uncircumcised when he received God's blessing? Paul writes:

Faith was accounted in the case of Abraham for his rectification. How then was it accounted? Was he circumcised or uncircumcised? He was not circumcised but was uncircumcised.

14. And, to reinforce that point, he associates Abraham with sinfulness. Verse 5 at least insinuates that Abraham was among the godless, and the Psalm text Paul introduces in vv. 7–8 pronounces a blessing on "the one [Abraham] whose sins are taken away."

Verse 11 reinforces this claim: "Abraham received a sign of circumcision as a seal of the rectification of faith he had *while he was still uncircumcised* so that he would be the father of all uncircumcised believers." When we find Paul explaining to the Romans that "Abraham was uncircumcised before he was circumcised," we know that he is not merely locating Abraham's circumcision on a timeline. He is emphasizing this fact. Verse 12 finally identifies Abraham as the "father of the circumcised" but then immediately qualifies that identification by insisting that he was not "the father only of circumcision." Although the Genesis narrative promises that Abraham will have offspring as numerous as the stars (Gen. 15:5; 22:17; 26:4; cf. Exod. 32:13; Deut. 1:10; 10:22; 28:62; 1 Chron. 27:23; Neh. 9:23; Sir. 44:20–21; Pr. Azar. 1:12–13), it is peculiar to find such priority given to gentile inheritance.[15]

Another peculiarity of this passage is that Paul makes no reference to the covenant as such. Notice again Romans 4:11: Abraham "received a sign of circumcision as a seal of the rectification of faith." Here Paul is drawing on the account of Abraham's circumcision in Genesis 17, but that account repeatedly refers to the covenant between God and Abraham. Circumcision itself is "a sign of the covenant between me and you" (Gen. 17:11).[16] Paul's infrequent use of the term "covenant" (here and elsewhere) does not suggest that God has given up the

---

15. Terence L. Donaldson, *Judaism and the Gentiles: Jewish Patterns of Universalism (to 135 CE)* (Waco: Baylor University Press, 2007), 499; Donaldson, *Paul and the Gentiles*, 126–28. Paul also makes no mention of a promise of land for Abraham's descendants. Given that Paul is writing to Rome and to an audience that, at the very least, contains a number of gentiles, who would have little or no interest in the land of Israel, that is understandable.

16. In fact, despite the easy way in which a number of scholars talk about Paul as a covenantal theologian, the word is rare in Paul's letters (appearing only at Rom. 9:4; 11:27; 1 Cor. 11:25; 2 Cor. 3:6, 14; Gal. 3:15, 17; 4:24). That silence is not determinative, but it does raise questions often neglected in the scholarly discussion. See the important essay by Francis Watson, "Is Paul a Covenantal Theologian?," in *The Unrelenting God: God's Action in Scripture; Essays in Honor of Beverly Roberts*

covenant, but perhaps Paul's preference for the term "promise" is revealing (as in Rom. 4:13–14, 16, 20; cf. Gal. 3–4). In this passage, the language of promise focuses on the seed, the offspring. What is important about the promise in Romans 4 is that God gave it, that Abraham acknowledged it with trust, and that it concerned offspring (prominently featuring gentile offspring). Isaac himself never makes an appearance, nor do any other of the ancient heirs of Abraham. Instead, there is a striking historical leap from the promise that Abraham trusted to the present time.

This leap from past to present appears dramatically in verse 17, which begins with a citation from Genesis 17:5: "I have appointed you [Abraham] to be father of many nations [gentiles]." In the presence of that promise, Paul explains, Abraham "believed God, who makes the dead live and who calls into being the things that do not exist." In one sense, this depiction of God fits the story of Isaac's birth quite well: Isaac did not exist before God called him into being, and Paul will shortly say that Abraham and Sarah were both so old they were practically dead (Rom. 4:19). But for Paul, of course, this way of speaking of God belongs most appropriately to God's raising of Jesus Christ from the dead. That point is confirmed in verse 24, when Paul writes that what is said about Abraham is also true for those who "believe in the one who raised Jesus our Lord from the dead." If our only source for the history of Israel were Romans 4, we would have to conclude that *nothing* happened between the time of Abraham and Sarah and the time of Paul and his Roman audiences.

Perhaps Paul simply assumes that his audiences will know the whole story and that they will unpack his brief summary,

Gaventa, ed. David J. Downs and Matthew L. Skinner (Grand Rapids: Eerdmans, 2013), 102–18.

supplying elements he has omitted.[17] If they do know Scripture, or at least know some elements of Abraham's story, such as the covenant with Abraham, the obedience of Abraham, and the founding of Israel through Abraham, then they will be in a position similar to that of the reader of the biography of Lincoln that passes over his childhood and the Emancipation Proclamation. They will be forced to think about this peculiar narration.

Often it is said that Paul tells this peculiar story of Abraham in order to offer him as an example of justification by faith.[18] That statement is accurate, but it can also mislead if it is taken to mean that Paul serves up Abraham's faith as an example of how to have faith or what to believe. Abraham certainly is said to be justified by faith, but very little in this passage suggests that Paul is encouraging the Roman audiences to believe like Abraham. Verse 12 is the strongest argument for Abraham as an example, since it identifies him as the father of those gentiles who walk in the steps of Abraham's faith. But that verse largely serves to associate Abraham further with gentile believers (as in v. 16) rather than to identify him as an example for emulation. Paul is perfectly capable of using mimetic language, and he does so with some regularity elsewhere:

> You became imitators of us and also of the Lord . . . so that you are an example for all who believe through Macedonia and Achaia. (1 Thess. 1:6–7)

17. This is one of the neuralgic points in contemporary Pauline study: What did Paul's audiences know of Scripture, and how did he expect them to hear his quotations and allusions? See footnote 11 above.

18. James D. G. Dunn, *Romans 1–8*, WBC 38A (Dallas: Word, 1988), 1:194–96, refers to Abraham as "a crucial test case" that "God justifies through faith" both Jews and gentiles. Robert Jewett, *Romans: A Commentary*, Hermeneia (Minneapolis: Fortress, 2007), 306, notes that Paul's comments fit both "a rabbinic pattern" and a Greco-Roman rhetorical method of providing "an *exemplum*" in order to appeal to both Jewish and Greco-Roman audiences.

I exhort you, therefore, be imitators of me. (1 Cor. 4:16)

Be imitators of me just as I am of Christ. (1 Cor. 11:1)

I plead with you, brothers and sisters, become like me, since I became like you. (Gal. 4:12)

Brothers and sisters, be imitators together of me, and take note of those who live by the example you have in us. (Phil. 3:17)

Whatever you have learned and received and heard and seen in me, do these things. (Phil. 4:9)

Paul could easily have written, "Believe as Abraham did" or "Look to Abraham as an example of faith." He did not do that. Instead, Abraham serves as an example of what God has done, not of Abraham's own character.

By the time we get to the end of the chapter, in fact, Abraham himself has faded away altogether and the argument returns to the present and to God's action in Jesus Christ. As Francis Watson has astutely observed, Abraham becomes a minor character in his own story.[19] On either translation of Romans 4:1, whether Abraham is the subject or "we" are, the question turns out to be a rhetorical "bait and switch." Abraham did not himself "find" anything; he was confronted by God's promise and trusted it. Nor do "we" find out anything about Abraham as "our fleshly ancestor"; we learn instead that God raised up offspring for Abraham because that is what God decided to do, both for Abraham and Sarah and for the entire cosmos. Abraham's story becomes the story of God's faith-generating actions for Abraham and, now, for all humankind (see v. 13, where Abraham's inheritance

19. Watson, *Paul and the Hermeneutics of Faith*, 179.

is the entire cosmos, and especially the cre̶ ̶ ̶ ̶ ̶ ̶ ̶
v. 17).

The leap Paul makes between past and pre̶ ̶ ̶ ̶
Romans 4 creates a significant gap in his argun ̶ ̶ ̶ ̶
immediately from Abraham's time to the pre̶ ̶ ̶ ̶
reference to any descendant between Isaac aɪɪu the present.
What is God doing with them? This is a question to which Paul
turns—at least in part—in chapters 9–11.

The Israel of God: Romans 9–11

In chapters 5–8, as we saw already in the first chapter, Paul
establishes the cosmic, universal horizon of the letter. God's
saving action in Jesus is needed for all humanity, because all are
enslaved to the powers of Sin and Death. And God's salvation
extends even beyond humanity, since the whole of creation
is said to be waiting for redemption (8:18–25). At the end of
chapter 8, Paul engages in something very like trash talk: Who
will condemn the humanity that God has acted in Christ to
save? Who or what can separate humanity from Christ's love?
The answer is emphatic: nothing. Nothing has the power to do
that. The list of possible contenders for destructive lordship in
8:38–39 is formidable. We are not certain what each item is or
represents, but at least some of these are cosmic forces: death
and life, angels and rulers, things that are and things that are
about to be, powers, height, depth, any other created thing.
Nothing can separate! Nothing outside of "us" can separate
"us from the love of God in Christ Jesus our Lord" (8:39).

There is one circumstance that Paul does not touch in Romans 8, however, and that is human rejection: Is it possible that
humanity can separate itself? Specifically, does Israel have the
power to remove itself from God's love? And if the answer to

question is yes, what does that suggest about God?[20] That question takes us, of course, to chapters 9–11.

Often 9:1–5 is read as a deeply emotional outcry on Paul's part, and there may well be some profound existential concerns involved in raising this set of questions. Emotion is hard to diagnose in a text, however. Think just of the perils involved in discerning the emotional temperature of an email message. How much more difficult is it to identify emotions in an author whose cultural repertoire is vastly removed from our own?[21]

Whatever the emotions at work in 9:1–5, these lines are pivotal as an entry into the larger discussion of God and Israel. One of the most important exegetical tasks is that of attending to the movement, the logic, the development of a text. That is true across the canon (or indeed outside the canon), and it is especially true with Paul. For Romans it is crucial. Too often, although we know better, as I noted in the introduction, we read this letter as if it were a collection of sayings, each of which bears the same weight in the argument as every other saying. We read as if each sentence or paragraph in the letter were a step on an escalator, doing exactly the same work as every other sentence or paragraph. But that strategy simply will not work. Paul is not writing a list of theological principles (however important his letters may be for our own

20. Wayne A. Meeks, "On Trusting an Unpredictable God: A Hermeneutical Meditation on Romans 9–11," in *Faith and History: Essays in Honor of Paul W. Meyer*, ed. John T. Carroll, Charles H. Cosgrove, and E. Elizabeth Johnson (Atlanta: Scholars Press, 1990), 105–24; reprinted in *In Search of the Early Christians: Selected Essays*, ed. Allen R. Hilton and H. Gregory Snyder (New Haven: Yale University Press, 2002), 210–29.

21. Ancient rhetoricians did engage in psychagogy, which involves a broadly therapeutic approach to human development (see the helpful overview in John A. Darr, "Narrative Therapy: Treating Audience Anxiety through Psychagogy in Luke," *PRSt* 39 [2012]: 335–48). What I have in mind here is not the practice of psychagogy but the attempt to read Paul's own emotional temperature.

theological views) or independent aphorisms. He is writing a letter, and in it he is constructing an argument. And as he develops his argument, sometimes he leads us down a path, only to show us that this particular path is a dead end. Or worse: the path leads us into an ambush.[22] Despite the impressive scholarly energy devoted to ancient rhetoric and Paul's use of ancient rhetoric, I do not think these twists and turns in Paul's letter have widely permeated our understanding of the letter.

In the case of Romans 9–11, the beginning and ending points of the discussion are clearly identified. In 9:1–5, Paul forcefully invokes God's gifts to Israel: the sonship, the glory, the covenants, the law, the worship, the promises, and so forth. The listing of gifts concludes with "God be blessed forever. Amen!" Paul also marks the culmination of this entire discussion at the end of chapter 11 with a series of Scripture texts and then another doxology: "From him and through him and to him are all things. To God be glory forever! Amen."[23]

Consistent with this emphasis on God's gifts to Israel and God as the creator of all things, the first half of chapter 9 establishes that Israel exists as and only as God's creation. Romans 9:6 reads (at least on my translation): "It is not as if God's word failed, for it is not the case that everyone who is from Israel constitutes Israel." That translation is admittedly unusual and requires a bit of explanation. A quite literal, and also quite unintelligible, translation would be: "Not all those from Israel, these Israel." The Greek has no verb, which means that translation into English permits—and indeed requires—the

---

22. Rom. 2:1 provides an especially apt example. Having stirred up his auditors with his sweeping indictment of the wrongdoing of others and declared "them" worthy of death itself, Paul then turns to attack the judgmental instinct of the auditors themselves.

23. The doxologies in Romans play an important role; see the discussion below in chap. 3.

insertion of some form of "is."[24] What form of "is" is appropriate? And what nuance is conveyed?

Many translations assume that Paul is making a distinction between Israelites by birth and some "real" or "true" or "spiritual" Israel. For example, the NRSV translates the verse as follows: "For not all Israelites *truly* belong to Israel," and the NET reads similarly: "For not all those who are descended from Israel are *truly* Israel" (emphasis added). The text, however, does not supply a modifier. And what follows in Paul's discussion has to do with bringing Israel into being in each generation, not with a "spiritual" versus a "physical" Israel. Instead of supplying an additional adjective or adverb that does not sit well with the argument, I have taken "is" to mean "constitute," as in "All the elected representatives are the Congress," which could equally read "All the elected representatives constitute the Congress" or "make up the Congress." Paul's is a negative form of that same statement, as in "It is not the case that the elected representatives constitute the Congress" or, in the case of 9:6, "It is not the case that all those who are from Israel constitute Israel."

What Paul conveys by that statement emerges only in the strange little history of Israel that follows, a history in which God repeatedly calls into being (that is, God creates) offspring for Abraham. These are biological children (this is the equivalent

---

24. This is standard Greek practice in which an equative verb—usually γίνομαι (*ginomai*), εἰμί (*eimi*), or ὑπάρχω (*hyparchō*) as a copula—needs to be supplied with the predicate nominative. See BDF §§127–28, 145; A. T. Robertson, *A Grammar of the Greek New Testament in the Light of Historical Research* (Nashville: Broadman, 1934), 395–96; Herbert Weir Smyth, *Greek Grammar* (Cambridge, MA: Harvard University Press, 1963), §§910–11, 944; Daniel B. Wallace, *Greek Grammar beyond the Basics: An Exegetical Syntax of the New Testament* (Grand Rapids: Zondervan, 1996), 40–48. Similar constructions, where the reader must supply a form of "is" in order to translate into intelligible English, appear at, e.g., John 1:23; 4:24; Rom. 2:8, 9–10; 3:1; 8:1, 7; 10:15; 1 Cor. 1:9, 24; 8:6; 10:13; 15:40; 2 Cor. 1:18; Eph. 4:4; Phil. 2:1; 4:5; 1 Thess. 2:5; 5:24.

of what is usually referred to as "ethnic" Israel),[25] but Paul's concern is with divine creation rather than with biology. In other words, Israel does not derive from itself. The Israel that exists is created by God and sustained by God for God's own purposes. *Israel exists not by virtue of its own faithfulness or goodness but by God's creative act.*[26]

That is to say: for Paul, Israel is God's. That simple conviction anchors everything that follows. All that follows is complicated, and at points it is perilous, but the twisted path repeatedly includes the suggestion that *Israel may be beyond rescue.* At numerous junctures, Paul dangles before his audience the possibility that Israel is beyond God's reach.

The first of these suggestions comes in 9:25–29, when Paul makes an audacious exegetical move. He calls on Hosea's language about God's creation of *Israel* in order to argue that *gentiles* are among God's people, that gentiles too are among the children of God:

I will call "not my people" my people,
and "not beloved" beloved.
And there, in the place where it was said to them,
"You are not my people,"
there they will be called the sons and daughters of
the living God. (Rom. 9:25–26)

25. I place "ethnic" in quotation marks to signal that ethnicity is also a socially constructed category, despite the fact that it often is treated as something biologically given. See Mark G. Brett, ed., *Ethnicity and the Bible*, BibInt 19 (New York: Brill, 1996); Denise Kimber Buell, *Why This New Race: Ethnic Reasoning in Early Christianity* (New York: Columbia University Press, 2005); Eric D. Barreto, *Ethnic Negotiations: The Function of Race and Ethnicity in Acts 16*, WUNT 2.294 (Tübingen: Mohr Siebeck, 2010).

26. Throughout the brief history of Israel in vv. 9–23, the emphasis lies on God's initiative. This emphasis extends even to the story of Pharaoh; where Scripture says both that God hardened Pharaoh's heart and that Pharaoh hardened his own heart, Paul mentions only God's role. See my essay "On the Calling-into-Being of Israel: Romans 9:6–29," in *Between Gospel and Election: Explorations in the Interpretation of Romans 9–11*, ed. Florian Wilk and J. Ross Wagner, WUNT 257 (Tübingen: Mohr Siebeck, 2010), 255–69.

In the context of Hosea 2, these words are addressed to Israel as God's beloved people who are promised both dire punishment and gracious redemption. These words that belong to Israel, Paul lifts from their native habitat and applies instead to gentiles. He then turns to Israel and writes that Isaiah "cried out" over Israel:

> Even if the number of the sons and daughters of Israel were as the sand of the sea, only a remnant will be saved. For the Lord will carry out his word on the earth fully and promptly. (Rom. 9:27–28)

He goes on, again calling on Isaiah's words:

> Unless the Lord of Hosts had left us offspring,
> we would have become Sodom
> and would have been like Gomorrah. (Rom. 9:29)

These lines already suggest that there will be a remnant, but the threat that comes to expression here is one of utter devastation.[27] There seems little reason for hope.

The elusive lines that follow scarcely alter the expectations. In 9:30–33, Paul contrasts Israel with the gentiles. While Israel has been running a race that it did not win, the gentiles have won a race they never entered. With chapter 10, Paul concedes that Israel has zeal for God but lacks understanding, despite the fact that the word of Christ is "near" and everyone who calls on the Lord's name will be saved. Israel has heard this word

27. See Wagner, *Heralds of the Good News*, 78–117. Wagner's analysis of Rom. 9:25–29 shows that the texts of both Hosea and Isaiah share linguistic correspondences as well as themes in their respective wider contexts. In his words, "through appropriating these prophetic promises of restoration after judgment for his own situation, Paul locates contemporary Israel in the same position as Isaiah's audience, between desolation and hope. In the present time, Israel suffers under the wrath of God and desperately needs to hear the message of reconciliation and release proclaimed by Isaiah—and now by Paul" (117).

of Christ, and God has relentlessly stretched out for God's people, but, as chapter 10 ends, God continues to reach out for "a disobedient and obstinate people."

All this argumentation drives Paul to the question of 11:1, "Has God rejected God's people?" That would seem to be the logical outcome of the argument: God is free to call Israel into being, and God is also free to execute judgment. Israel has heard the message but has not responded. Israel has remained disobedient even in the face of God's pleading. God must have rejected God's people!

But even before Paul's characteristic answer, "Of course not!" the question bears within it its own negation. Paul introduces it with the Greek particle *mē* indicating that a negative answer will follow. So the question is better translated as, "It's not really that God has rejected God's people, is it?" Even without Greek grammar, however, the point is clear: Has God rejected God's people? The instant Paul refers to Israel as *"God's* people," he already suggests the impossibility of any notion that God rejects Israel.

Paul is not finished. There is yet another stage in the argument, since it is not enough to say that God does not "reject." Where is the evidence for God's non-rejection, and where will that non-rejection lead? In 11:1b–10, Paul contends that there is a remnant, just as there was in the day of Elijah, a remnant established only by grace. Verses 5–6 repeatedly insist that it is God's grace that establishes the remnant:

So also in the present time, a remnant has come about through grace, according to [God's] calling. And since it is by grace, it is not any longer based on works, since then grace would no longer be grace.

In addition to this "remnant" called into being by grace, there are "the rest." Here again Paul calls on Scripture to reinforce his point: God established this "rest" by giving them a spirit that does not understand, eyes that do not see, ears that will not hear, even until the present day. Just as the "remnant" exists by virtue of God's action, so do the "rest" stand hardened by God's action. Israel is divided between the "remnant" and the "rest." This division could mean that there is a part of Israel that is the "real" Israel and a part of Israel that is—or will be—lost, which is how many interpreters have read Romans 9–11. The question of 11:11 faces that possibility: Is their fall permanent? And the answer is as emphatic as the answers to earlier, equally preposterous questions in the letter:[28] "Of course not!" Paul contends that the temporary stumble of "the rest" serves God's purpose. God is using this division in Israel—a division God created—to bring in the gentiles. (For now I am setting aside the crucial address to gentiles in vv. 13–24 in order to stay close to the argument about Israel. I will return to that address below.)

In 11:25, Paul comes finally to the point to which he has been driving all along: a divinely induced hardening has come on part of Israel temporarily in order to bring about the faith of the gentiles. Then "all Israel will be saved" (v. 26). There is a long and tortured history of debating exactly what Paul means by the expression "all Israel."[29] If that debate did not carry such disastrous implications, it might be amusing. It is as if we cannot quite comprehend what the simple word "all" might mean (and I will have more to say about this point in the conclusion to this book). Some have argued that it refers only to the "believing remnant" of Israel, others that it refers to the church (i.e., both Jews and gentiles who believe in Jesus). Given the division that Paul posits earlier between the "remnant" and

28. E.g., Rom. 3:3–4, 5–6, 31; 6:1–2, 15; 7:7, 13; 9:14; 11:1.
29. For a helpful review of the discussion, see Christopher Zoccali, "'And So All Israel Will Be Saved': Competing Interpretations of Romans 11:26 in Pauline Scholarship," *JSNT* 30 (2008): 289–318.

"the rest," it seems likely that "all Israel" refers to the whole of Israel. It is the same group that we label "ethnic" or "biological" or "historical" Israel, except that, for Paul, Israel is not an anthropological but a theological category.

There may well never be exegetical agreement on this point, but however we understand "all Israel," what follows is crucial, as here Paul begins to unpack this statement. Verses 26–31 tersely restate what Paul has already said since the beginning of chapter 11. If part of Israel is at enmity with God, that situation exists so that God may have mercy on gentiles. That part of Israel nonetheless is beloved by God and remains so: "The gifts and the calling of God are unchanging" (v. 29). Verse 32 then recasts the statement that "all Israel will be saved" into language that extends to all of humanity: "God confined all to disobedience so that God might have mercy on all." If such a sweeping claim seems impossible, Paul punctuates it with yet another series of scriptural quotations. All of these are about the impossibility of humanity knowing, controlling, predicting, repaying, or otherwise influencing God.

As with the peculiar narration of Abraham's story in chapter 4, it is important to notice both what Paul says about Israel and what he does not say. Paul does not say that "all Israel" will believe. He does not say that the people of Israel will confess and thereby be saved. Verse 23 might seem to be an exception, with its assertion that if "they" do not persist in unbelief, they will be grafted in again, but even that verse does not quite say that they *will* believe. What he says is:

Israel will be saved: the saving one is God.
God's gifts and God's calling are unchanging.
God confined all to disobedience, that God might have mercy.
God's ways are not known to human beings.

That is to say: Paul has shifted the subject once again. He has continually raised a question about Israel and its conduct, and he has continually answered that question by reference to God. It turns out that the question of Israel is not a question about Israel. It is a question about God.

Some interpreters would welcome what I have just said, but they would go on to add something like, "Of course. Paul knows that God is the God of Israel." Here's the curious part: that is an expression Paul never uses. Neither in Romans nor in any other letter does Paul speak of the "God of Israel" (cf. Matt. 15:31; Luke 1:68),[30] or the "God of Abraham" (or "of Abraham, Isaac, and Jacob"; cf. the citation of Exod. 3:6 in Mark 12:26 and parallels; Acts 3:13; 7:32), or the "God of our fathers" (Acts 3:13; 7:32).[31] We find those expressions in the Gospels, in the Septuagint, in other Jewish and Christian texts of the period, but not in Paul. Instead, at the very point where some reference to "the God of Abraham" or "the God of our fathers" might be expected, Paul identifies God as "the one who raised Jesus our Lord from the dead" (Rom. 4:24). That silence is far from self-interpreting, and I do not pretend to know whether Paul self-consciously made this decision. At the very least, it is consistent with the understanding that, for Paul, Israel belongs to God but not God to Israel. Israel is not proprietary over God; God is proprietary over Israel.

Perhaps this is a false distinction. It could be objected that no one ever claimed that "the God of Israel" is a genitive of

30. Rom. 3:29 does include the question, "Is God of the Jews only?" but there the phrase does not appear to function as a name or title. Instead it functions as a statement of possession, as in "Does God have to do with Jews only?"

31. "God of Israel" does appear in the LXX (e.g., Exod. 24:10; Josh. 7:13; Judg. 4:6; 5:3; 6:8; 2 Esd. 1:3 [Ezra 1:3]; Tob. 13:17; 2 Macc. 9:5; Sir. 47:18; Isa. 41:17; 45:3; Jer. 16:9; Bar. 2:11) and also in early Jewish and Christian texts (e.g., Prot. Jas. 6.2; 14.2; 16.2; 4 Bar. 6:20; Jos. Asen. 7:5). For examples of "God of Abraham" or "God of Jacob" or "of Isaac," see LXX Gen. 28:13; 32:10; Pss. 23:6; 45:8, 12; 74:10; 83:9; Isa. 2:3.

possession—that is, "Israel's God," as in "Israel possesses God."
And that may well be true. In one sense, the use of that phrase
"the God of Israel" merely invokes the history of God's actions
with this particular people. I am not advocating that we give
up the phrase. I do think, however, that some contemporary
developments in Pauline studies imply that we should be able
to extrapolate from Israel's history into Paul's letters, that Paul
does not say anything distinctive, that he stands in exactly the
same line as his predecessors. Yet when Paul calls God a name,
it is "the one who raised Jesus our Lord from the dead" or "the
Father of our Lord Jesus Christ."

The better way to express the possession is with "the Israel
of God." The only Israel that exists, for Paul, is the one that
God called into being with the promise to Abraham, the one
that God redeems—along with the gentiles—with Jesus Christ,
and the one to whom God's promises are unbreakable.[32] Does
that mean that Paul thinks eventually Israel too will confess
Jesus as Lord? That Israel will believe? How Paul would answer
that question is unclear, and the end of chapter 11 may mean
he knows that the answer remains hidden within God's own
unknowability.

How different the church's history would be had that question been left to God.

Questions That Linger

On this reading—in fact, on most any reading of Romans 9–11—
it is a peculiar argument. How does Paul arrive at the notion that
God is using Jewish unbelief, indeed, that God has *brought about*
Jewish unbelief, in order to save gentiles, so that God may in turn

32. On that phrase and its valence in Paul, see Susan Grove Eastman, "Israel
and the Mercy of God: A Re-reading of Galatians 6.16 and Romans 9–11," *NTS*
56 (2010): 367–95.

save Jews? Is this a result of his study of Scripture? Has he taken the prophetic understanding of eschatological pilgrimage and turned it upside down?[33] Does the fact that he calls it a mystery in 11:25 suggest that he has received it by divine revelation? Does he know at the outset of chapter 9 where the argument will go? Or does he discover his conclusions along the way?

The latter suggestion, that Paul discovers his conclusions along the way, is attractive, particularly for Christians who themselves search Scripture for insight into new problems. Yet the whole of Romans is so carefully constructed, with intricate connections across the length of the letter, that it seems unlikely that he "discovered" his position while writing the letter as we have it. (He may have "discovered" his position in the process of conversation with others following the crisis in the Galatian churches, but that is another scenario altogether.) The letter we have is not a first draft.

Yet if Paul knows where the argument will go when he begins writing (or better: dictating) the letter, why the prolonged and complex argument? Why not say what he wants to say more directly? The answer to that question probably comes into view with 11:13, "I am speaking to you gentiles." No longer content with third-person depictions of God's dealings with Israel, Paul

33. Some readers of Paul's letter see in chap. 11 elements related to the "eschatological pilgrimage" motif. "Eschatological pilgrimage" refers to the notion that at the end of days Israel will experience a full restoration and, as a result, a number of gentiles will be ushered into Jerusalem. Some texts, however, envision the judgment and destruction of gentiles rather than their redemption. On this topic see Donaldson, *Paul and the Gentiles*, 69–74; Donaldson, *Judaism and the Gentiles*, 499–505; E. P. Sanders, *Jesus and Judaism* (Philadelphia: Fortress, 1985), 77–119; Sanders, *Judaism: Practice and Belief 63 BCE–66 CE* (London: SCM, 1992), 291–92. Previously I have argued that if this is the case, then Paul overturns that tradition in two primary ways. First, it is the failure of Israel that leads to gentile inclusion, and second, the gentiles now take the lead in bringing about Israel's redemption; see "The God Who Will Not Be Taken for Granted: Reflections on Paul's Letter to the Romans," in *The Ending of Mark and the Ends of God: Essays in Memory of Donald Harrisville Juel*, ed. Beverly Roberts Gaventa and Patrick D. Miller (Louisville: Westminster John Knox, 2005), 83.

turns to address the party whose argument is at fault. Paul's concern is not that most of Israel doesn't believe Jesus to be the Messiah and therefore will suffer the consequences. His concern is with those gentile Christians who have themselves drawn that conclusion. Gentiles think that they have displaced Israel, or at the very least they think that Israel's unwillingness to acknowledge Jesus as the rightful Messiah of God means that God will reject Israel (at least part of Israel).

In order to bring the audience to his conclusion, Paul moves with great care, showing repeatedly that Israel (like the gentiles) has always existed only out of God's own creative and sustaining action.

Admittedly, this depiction of gentile Christians in the first century is somewhat speculative. But it is not speculation to observe that gentile Christians after Paul, even in the twenty-first century, have read him in just this way, presuming to have the mind of God (11:34), presuming to know who belongs to the root and who does not, presuming to understand the reach and grasp of God's calling, God's grace. To such gentiles—then and now—the emphatic words of 11:29 resound: the gifts and the calling of God are irrevocable.

The "So What" Question

Donald Juel, a New Testament scholar whose voice we lost much too soon, was fond of posing the provocative question: "What is this good for?" By way of conclusion, I will ask that question of Romans 4 and 9–11. In *our* time, what is this discussion of Abraham and of Israel good for?

To state only the most obvious conclusion, I hope it is "good for" combating the church's constant temptation to anti-Judaism. What we see in Romans consistently is that Jews and gentiles have differing histories with God, but all alike are subject to the powers of Sin and Death. Gentile (i.e., in our time, Christian) arrogance violates *both* our shared sinfulness *and* God's history with Israel. "Do not boast over the root!" comes Paul's clear word in 11:18.

I long for the day when that word does not need to be said.

But I also want to note, albeit briefly, the way Paul is working, both here and elsewhere. On most any reading of Romans, Paul is faced with a serious ecclesial problem concerning the relationship between Jewish and gentile Christians. He might just say, "Well, be nice to one another. You can have separate congregations, each of whom will witness to its own constituency, and that witness will spread the gospel." More likely, he might have said, "The growing market is with gentile Christians, so forget Israel." Instead of simply trying to patch the problem or even to find a viable practical solution, he *first* thinks about God. What is God up to? What has God done in Jesus? What does that teach us? To be sure, he concludes with a doxology in which he hands the problem back to God, but not before thinking long and hard about where God is in the current crisis.

The same thing happens elsewhere: as we will see in chapter 4, in Romans 14 Paul invokes God's lordship to think about how to have a community meal when some folks are vegans and others are omnivores. In 1 Corinthians 11, he invokes the cross of Jesus as he tries to discern how the Lord's Supper is to be celebrated across social differences: the wealthy show up first and drink all the wine; the slaves show up last and go hungry. In 1 Thessalonians 4, he invokes the return of Jesus as he addresses the inescapable human fact of grief.

He does not back away from any of these practical problems, but he first thinks about any and all of them through the lens of God's determination to redeem the world from itself. May we learn the same lesson!

3

WHEN IN ROMANS . . .
GIVE GLORY TO GOD

When I first began teaching in a theological school many years ago, I regularly made use of a fine little book by Robin Scroggs, *Paul for a New Day*. In the preface, Scroggs explains that the book began as lectures for pastors. He recalls that, while teaching a continuing education course for pastors, he gave a first lecture that was focused entirely on the new being brought into existence by God's action in Jesus Christ. He made no reference to questions of human response or human behavior, saving that for his last lecture. Yet following the first lecture, he was immediately "bombarded by a number of very serious questioners," all of whom were concerned with human action. "But you didn't tell us what to do!"[1]

That story rings true for my own teaching experience as well, and I think the reasons (or some of them) for the persistent

1. Robin Scroggs, *Paul for a New Day* (Philadelphia: Fortress, 1977), viii.

75

demand, "Tell us what to do!" are good ones. We are—rightly—worried about cheap grace. We are—rightly—eager to find guidelines for our lives and especially for the lives of our children. We are—rightly—concerned that Paul's gospel smacks of "pie in the sky by and by," which demands nothing in the present. The same logic prompted Howard Thurman's grandmother to warn him against reading the letters of Paul, which she regarded as dangerous.[2] We want to counter the charge that Paul's letters are remote and abstract, and one way to do that is to ask, "What do we do?"

Here we enter the neighborhood conventionally identified as "Pauline ethics." And, as with the discussions of salvation and of Israel in earlier chapters, here it is expected that we will ask certain sorts of questions. Probably the most persistent question in Pauline ethics concerns what is referred to as the relationship between the "indicative" and the "imperative." These terms are shorthand references to the relationship between Paul's understanding of God's action in Jesus Christ and the ethical instructions he offers. The discussion revolves around trying to distinguish how these two bodies of material intersect, intermingle, and inform each other. For instance, does the indicative (i.e., an account of the gospel) amount to an offer that is secured by the imperative (i.e., human conduct)? Or is the imperative tied more intrinsically, more naturally, to the indicative so that they are difficult to distinguish from each other?[3] Is Paul saying, "Become what you are," as it is often understood? Or does he mean something more like "become what you are becoming"?[4]

---

2. Howard Thurman, *Jesus and the Disinherited* (1940; repr., Richmond, IN: Friends United Press, 1981), 30.

3. For an important example of this view, see Victor Paul Furnish, *Theology and Ethics in Paul*, NTL (1968; repr., Louisville: Westminster John Knox, 2009), 224–27.

4. James D. G. Dunn, *Romans 1–8*, WBC 38A (Dallas: Word, 1988), 337. See Udo Schnelle's discussion of the difficulty of this way of putting things, in *Apostle Paul:*

When we turn to specific ethical instructions in the Pauline letters, we encounter a host of questions: Where do these instructions come from? Many of them have parallels elsewhere in ancient literature, in either Jewish or non-Jewish texts or both. In Romans in particular, one of the perennial discussions has to do with the law of Moses, because Paul makes a number of comments about the law, and they are, to put it mildly, not easily reconciled with one another.[5] Scholars debate the place of the law in Paul's understanding of the Christian life and how it continues to be a factor in Paul's ethical instructions.

What prompts Paul to offer certain ethical instructions? And what do his teachings have to do with the particular contexts in which Paul writes? Romans 14, for example, takes up disputes over the observance or nonobservance of Jewish food law (a feature of the Mosaic law just mentioned). The issue is how Christians conduct themselves when there are disputes about questions as practical as which foods belong or do not belong on the common table. Details in this passage might help us to understand better what Christianity looked like in Rome in this very early period and also shed light on the rest of the letter. Another example comes with Romans 13:1–7, which instructs believers to be "submissive" to the governing authorities: What is it that prompts this teaching (one that does not occur elsewhere in Paul's letters)? Such questions are especially hard to answer in Romans, where Paul has not visited the Christian communities he addresses and where he must be cautious in the way he presents his views.

Perhaps most important for those of us who are committed to teach and preach Paul's letters is the question of how his ethical teachings relate to our own contexts. How do we

---

His Life and Theology, trans. M. Eugene Boring (Grand Rapids: Baker Academic, 2003), 546–51.

5. See the discussion of this problem in chap. 2 above.

interpret them today in Christian communities? Can his comments in Romans 14 about different practices regarding food shed light on our own negotiation of differences within Christian communities? What is to be learned, if anything at all, from Romans 13:1–7? In recent decades, of course, intense Christian disputes about homosexuality have relentlessly discussed Paul's comments in Romans 1 about same-sex relations (on which see below). Can Paul's model of negotiating differences helpfully inform contemporary Christian engagement with hotly contested disputes?

These complex and challenging questions recur in one form or another in most discussions of Paul's ethics.[6] In this chapter, rather than addressing any of these conventional questions about ethics, I will again contend, as I have in earlier chapters, that our readings are too limited. Specifically, our thinking about Paul's ethics is somewhat constricted. We have become preoccupied with answering individual questions at the expense of following the letter's own developing logic. If we do follow its logic, we may well find that *the best starting place for thinking about how "we" live is to think about worship.*

Those schooled in customary ways of thinking about ethics may find this a strange starting point, perhaps even an alternative topic altogether. In seminaries, worship and ethics are usually two different fields of study, two different courses, two different subject matters that seldom come together. In local congregations, the word "worship" refers to what happens at a particular hour on Sunday morning. "Ethics," on the other

6. A vast scholarly literature treats these questions; see especially Furnish, *Theology and Ethics in Paul*; Richard B. Hays, *The Moral Vision of the New Testament: A Contemporary Introduction to New Testament Ethics* (San Francisco: HarperOne, 1996); and David G. Horrell, *Solidarity and Difference: A Contemporary Reading of Paul's Ethics*, 2nd ed. (London: T&T Clark, 2015). A nontechnical volume that treats some controversial issues with care is Victor Paul Furnish, *The Moral Teaching of Paul: Selected Issues*, 3rd ed. (Nashville: Abingdon, 2009).

hand, refers to the content of an adult education forum where we discuss some hot-button issue, or perhaps to our participation in local mission programs.

In addition, when we make our periodic visits to Romans, we go in search of Christian doctrine rather than worship. If we want Paul's help in thinking about worship, we look to 1 Corinthians 11–14, where he comments on the observance of the Eucharist and offers some straightforward advice about how to conduct a service of worship in a way that honors the spiritual gifts of some people without making the service into a spectacle. Yet worship is deeply engrained in the fabric of this letter, as we can see even in the opening of what is usually referred to as the "ethical" section of the letter.

"Throw Your Bodies in the Offering Plate": Romans 12:1–2

The place to begin is with 12:1–2, which ranks high on the hit parade of most familiar texts from Romans. It graces many continuing education brochures and frequently appears as a slogan for youth retreats:

> Therefore I encourage you, brothers and sisters, through God's mercies, to present your bodies as a sacrifice—living, holy, acceptable to God. That is your reasonable worship. And do not be conformed to this age, but be transformed through the renewal of your mind-set, so that you may discern what is God's will—the good and acceptable and fully mature.

This admonition is something of a turning point in the letter. It follows immediately on the end of the discussion in Romans 9–11 about God's dealings with Israel (and the gentiles), and it introduces the "ethical section" of the letter. It offers a lens through which we may read and interpret the remainder of the letter body. Here Paul addresses Roman Christians as people who have been released from their captivity to Sin by God's action in Jesus Christ. No longer incapacitated by Sin and Death, they are, by God's merciful intervention, empowered to act. Verse 2 encapsulates the move: no longer constrained by "this age" but enabled by a new mind-set, a new mind, they are able to discern God's will.

But what of the first verse: present your *bodies* as a sacrifice—living, holy, pleasing to God, your reasonable worship? Since popular views hold Paul responsible for introducing negative attitudes toward the human body into Christian thought, it is worth pausing here to notice that he uses the word "body" (in Greek, *sōma*, as in "somatic") to refer to the whole person. The "body" is the physical body, as when he writes in Galatians 6:17, "I bear the marks of Christ in my body." More than physicality alone is involved, however, especially when Paul speaks of the church as Christ's own body (as in Rom. 12:4–5 and more extensively in 1 Cor. 12). To urge his auditors to present their "bodies" is to say: "Present yourselves, all that there is of you."

This comment, in and of itself, powerfully rebuffs the fear that Paul's understanding of "grace" is actually nothing more than "cheap grace."[7] In this passage, it emerges that for Paul grace is both utterly free and utterly costly: it demands everything. The same understanding comes to expression when he speaks, as he does only a few times, of his own conversion or his calling to apostolic service. In Philippians 3 he provides a brief résumé of his credentials prior to his conversion. He begins with attributes that came to him by birth or by the action of his family and moves on to his own dispositions: he

---

7. On grace in Paul's thought, see now the masterful work of John M. G. Barclay, *Paul and the Gift* (Grand Rapids: Eerdmans, 2015).

was a Pharisee, sufficiently zealous that he "persecuted"[8] the church, and he was blameless in the sight of the Mosaic law (Phil. 3:5–7). He then immediately claims also that all those indications of his own status have been lost to him. In fact, he regards them as excrement because he was overtaken by Christ (3:8, 12). The gospel cost him everything. Paul makes such statements—Galatians 1:11–17 is another—not to broadcast his own spiritual journey as a Facebook update but to offer an instance of the gospel's impact. It brings about nothing less than new creation (2 Cor. 5:17; Gal. 6:15). When Paul calls for giving over the whole person, he does so in the dialect of worship. "To present a sacrifice" is technical terminology found elsewhere in Paul's world.[9] Paul goes on to write that this offering is "your reasonable worship." The NRSV reads "spiritual" worship (Rom. 12:1), but that translation is misleading, since it can suggest (at least for North American Christians) something that is interior, private, perhaps even unreal. This worship is, as Paul sees it, reasonable: it is fitting to the actions of God.

Paul further says that this sacrifice is "living, holy, acceptable to God" (Rom. 12:1). Sometimes this admonition, and especially these last words, is reduced to a polemic against the Jewish sacrificial system or perhaps against animal sacrifice in general[10] (which was practiced both in Jewish and in non-Jewish

---

8. The scare quotes around "persecuted" reflect an attempt to suggest that Paul's action may have been verbal rather than violent; see Beverly Roberts Gaventa, *From Darkness to Light: Aspects of Conversion in the New Testament* (Philadelphia: Fortress, 1986), 17–51.

9. See the examples provided in Walter Bauer, Frederick William Danker, W. F. Arndt, and F. W. Gingrich, eds., *A Greek-English Lexicon of the New Testament and Other Early Christian Literature*, 3rd ed. (Chicago: University of Chicago Press, 2000), 462–63.

10. Arland J. Hultgren, *Paul's Letter to the Romans: A Commentary* (Grand Rapids: Eerdmans, 2011), 439–40; Ernst Käsemann, *Commentary on Romans*, trans. and ed. Geoffrey W. Bromiley (Grand Rapids: Eerdmans, 1980), 326–29. See also James D. G. Dunn, *Romans 9–16*, WBC 38B (Dallas: Word, 1988), 708–11.

religious traditions). Yet that argument does not fit the evidence of Paul's letters. To begin with, Paul does not elsewhere polemicize against the use of animal sacrifice. The book of Hebrews does at great length compare the sacrifice of Jesus with that of the Jerusalem temple, but such comparisons are remote from Paul.[11] Also, Paul has just completed a long, complex, careful account of God's dealings with Israel, which begins by listing God's gifts to Israel, including worship (9:4), and culminates with the emphatic assertion that God's gifts and calling do not change (11:29). It would seem rather counterproductive for him immediately to throw an elbow in the direction of Jewish worship practices.

Transforming this passage into a polemic against other religious traditions is a convenient way of keeping the text at arm's length. By refusing to hear Paul's radical claim that genuine worship involves returning to God what is God's, which means the whole person, we once again reduce the text to something small, manageable, malleable. Instead of some domesticated message we can handle, Romans 12:1–2 meets us with the intimidating notion that there is no limit to God's claims on us.

Parallel readings elsewhere are easy to come by. In Luke 20, Jesus responds to a tricky question about whether it is "lawful" to pay taxes to Caesar. He says, "Repay Caesar what is Caesar's and God what is God's" (20:25; and see Mark 12:17; Matt. 22:21). In many churches, this instruction becomes a proof text for the necessity of paying taxes or perhaps paying both taxes and the church pledge. Yet Luke (together with Mark and Matthew) knows that everything belongs to God, the creator of all that exists and the one who sends his son on behalf of Israel's redemption and the salvation of the world. To reduce

11. In Rom. 3:25, Paul does identify Christ with the "mercy seat" in a verse that is among the more hotly contested in the letter. It is quite a stretch, however, to read that passage as an argument against the sacrificial system.

Jesus's statement to advice about tax paying is to shrink God's arena to that which is tidy, convenient, inoffensive.

The net effect of Romans 12:1 is to place Christian living within the sphere of worship. The doxology that concludes Romans 11 amplifies the liturgical effect: "From him and through him and for him are all things. To God be the glory forever. Amen!" As Phoebe reads the letter aloud to gatherings of Christians in Rome, that exclamation may well prompt a response from the hearers: "Amen!" (I will have more to say about this response below.) And then they hear that they—their persons— are the sacrifice, the appropriate act of worship.

This slender text introducing Paul's ethical instructions is no mere polemic against other people's religious practice. Nor is Paul simply making his argument more vivid by using liturgical language. For Paul, there is an integral relationship between worship and what we call ethics. In order to see that connection, we need to reach back all the way to the opening of the letter, where Paul announces that the gospel reveals both God's salvation and God's wrath.

Worship and Conduct Intertwined and Corrupted

In Romans 1:18 Paul writes, "The wrath of God has been revealed apocalyptically from heaven against all ungodliness and wrong of human beings who suppress the truth with wrong." He then unpacks at some length what he means by this assertion (extending at least through vv. 19–32). Many questions occupy the scholarly discussion of this passage, including its function in the letter and the influences that shape Paul's argument. Verses 26–27 have been among the major focal points of discussion regarding the Bible and human sexuality, specifically same-sex relations. The intense interest in this text is understandable, given the deep disagreements about homosexuality that have preoccupied North American Christianity in recent decades.

Yet just as shining a spotlight on a stage leaves the rest of the stage in near darkness, putting a huge spotlight on two verses has obscured the rest of this passage. Indeed, directing that spotlight toward these two verses distorts even those verses, since it tempts readers to think that Paul's only real concern is with sexual conduct.[12]

What often falls into shadow in all the debate about homosexuality, most unfortunately, is Paul's claim that the problem generating all other problems is the withholding of worship from God. Paul begins with the sweeping announcement that God's wrath is being revealed apocalyptically against "all ungodliness and wrong of human beings who suppress the truth with wrong" (v. 18). As he begins to explain what he means, he writes that "they" had knowledge about God that was revealed to them, but they "did not glorify God as God or give God thanks" (v. 21). He goes on to say that, because of their foolishness, they "exchanged the glory of the imperishable God with the likeness of the image of a perishable human being— and birds, and four-footed things—and even reptiles!" (v. 23). For this reason, he continues, "God handed them over." Three times he makes the same statement: God handed them over (vv. 24, 26, 28).[13] Following his statement about the handing over of "them," Paul adduces the practice of sexuality out of control, as well as the practices of greed, envy, guile, gossip, and numerous others. It is important to attend to the list, because we have so obsessed about Paul's sexual references that we overlook the full content of the list. (Anyone who thinks she or he is exempt

12. Those who want to read further about vv. 26–27 will be helped by Furnish, *Moral Teaching of Paul*, 55–93, and Hays, *Moral Vision*, 379–406.

13. On the "handing over" and its significance in Romans, see Beverly Roberts Gaventa, *Our Mother Saint Paul* (Louisville: Westminster John Knox, 2007), 113–23.

from the charges in this section of the letter needs to read vv. 29–32 again, perhaps more slowly.)

The logic of the passage is clear. All the practices Paul excoriates *result from* refusing to worship God and treating created things as if they were God. He is talking about idolatry, but the problem with Christian use of that term in the present is that we think it does not have anything to do with us.

In other words, there is for Paul a firm connection between worship and behavior. Withholding worship, which is what he means when he speaks of not glorifying God and not giving God thanks, is the *cause* of a host of distorted practices. The unstated corollary is that the right praise of God is the condition—and indeed the only possible condition—for right conduct.[14]

It is possible, of course, to read or hear 1:18–32 and conclude that Paul is talking about someone else. He appears to invite his audience to do just that, because he never identifies the "they," which of course leaves his audience to imagine that they (we) are not included. Because his remarks resemble the anti-gentile polemics found in some early Jewish literature,[15] it is possible to conclude that Paul is talking only about gentiles—about pagans.[16] It is not difficult to imagine how Paul's words could be understood:

> Come on. We all know about them. Everyone knows they are the people who worship anything and everything. And you know they eat anything and they sleep with anyone.

14. That "condition" of worship, in Paul's view, can be arrived at only by God's action in Jesus Christ, which is the deliverance discussed in chap. 1 above.

15. This is scarcely a one-sided polemic. On gentile slander against Jews, see the texts collected in Menahem Stern, ed., *Greek and Latin Authors on Jews and Judaism*, 3 vols. (Jerusalem: Israel Academy of Science and Humanities, 1974–84).

16. For examples of anti-gentile polemic in Jewish literature that share similarities with Rom. 1:18–32, see Wis. 11:15–16; 12:24; 13:1–10; 15:1–16:1.

We hear the offspring of this language on a regular basis:

> They are the people who expect to get a handout without doing any work. They sit at home and watch television while we go to work. They drive to the grocery in new cars and buy frozen dinners with their food stamps. We know about them.

Paul will have none of this habit of finding fault in the other and overlooking our own failings (not to mention Jesus's own warnings, as in Matt. 7:1–5). In Romans 2, he works to undermine any assumption that the human problem lies elsewhere, that it lies in others and has nothing to do with us. His path is somewhat circuitous, but it drives on to 3:9, to the conclusion that all people, without exception, are under the power of Sin. At that point, in 3:10–18, Paul includes a catena, which is a technical term referring to something like a mash-up composed of lines drawn from several different biblical texts. In this case, most of the texts come from the Psalms.

The effect of the catena is to bring this entire section of the letter to a close with the emphatic claim that no one does what is right. The catena reinforces at least some of the comments in 1:18–32. It opens with these lines:

> There is not a righteous one, not even one,
> There is not one who understands.
> There is not one who seeks God. (3:10–11)

And it closes similarly:

> They do not know the way of peace.
> There is no fear of God before their eyes. (3:17–18)

To be sure, Paul is not speaking here about worship in the narrow sense of a formal act of liturgy offered during a set time in a fixed location. He does not, as he does in Romans 1, speak specifically of giving thanks to God or praising God. Nonetheless, the broader sense of worship as the rightful acknowledgment of the creator by the creature comes to expression again here, particularly in the claim that there is no one who seeks God (drawn from Ps. 14), that there is no one who fears God (drawn from Ps. 36).

Connecting the catena more tightly to 1:18–32, Paul couples this forceful claim about the absence of worship with particular charges about misconduct:

> All have turned away, together they have become
>   worthless.
> There is not even one who does the good,
> There is not even one. (3:12)

The middle of the catena makes some specific charges about vile speech and human violence:

> An opened grave is their throat,
> with their tongues they deceive,
> the venom of asps is under their lips;
> their mouth is filled with cursing and bitterness,
> swift are their feet for shedding blood,
> destruction and wretchedness are in their paths.
>   (3:13–16)

The catena does not explicitly make the logical connection apparent in chapter 1, where the argument suggests that the withholding of worship—the distortion of worship—prompts God to hand humanity over, with the result that it falls into the behavior Paul castigates. Constructed as it is from a variety of Psalm texts, the catena would not readily lend itself to the argumentative moves of chapter 1.[17] Nonetheless, there is at least an association forged in the catena between the failure to honor God and reprehensible conduct. And that association between the refusal to worship God and immorality is allowed to stand by way of both extending and reinforcing what Paul has said from 1:18 forward: "there is not one" who escapes the intertwined charges of godlessness (worshiplessness) and immorality. In other words, worship and behavior are integrally related.

What is under the surface in 1:18–3:20—namely, the power of Sin itself—comes into full view when we reach Romans 5–7 (as discussed already in chap. 1 above regarding the scope of Sin's [and Death's] grasp of humanity). In that section of the letter, Paul's language has less to do with worship than it does with the death-dealing power of Sin and the even more triumphant power of Grace. In chapter 4, Paul does mention that Abraham gave glory to God (something he has not said earlier about anyone else). And in chapter 5 he writes, "We were ungodly."

Worship and Conduct Re-created

We have seen that the early chapters of Romans portray a negative relationship between worship and ethics: the absence of worship or the distortion of worship produces corrupt behavior. Thus, in chapter 8, finally, Paul turns away from his depiction of the power of Sin and takes up the power of the Spirit. And it is in chapter 8 that we learn how the worship of God, which had been withheld by humans and corrupted by Sin, is enabled as a

17. For further discussion of the composition and function of the catena, see Beverly Roberts Gaventa, "From Toxic Speech to the Redemption of Doxology in Paul's Letter to the Romans," in *The Word Leaps the Gap: Essays on Scripture and Theology in Honor of Richard B. Hays*, ed. J. Ross Wagner, C. Kavin Rowe, and A. Katherine Grieb (Grand Rapids: Eerdmans, 2008), 392–408.

result of the arrival of the gospel in the death and resurrection of Jesus Christ. It is because "we" have received the Spirit that we are able to cry out, "Abba, Father!" (8:15). "We" receive the fruit of worship by the intercession of the Spirit, and we are nurtured by the Spirit, who intercedes for us (8:23, 26). "We" cry out, together with the whole of creation and against and in spite of the continuing efforts of the anti-God powers (8:22–23). Thus, as Paul takes up the work of the Spirit, human worship is reborn in the cry to God.

Romans is often thought to be all about theology, and what I classify as worship in Romans 1–3 some interpreters may regard as having to do with theology or faith rather than with worship as such. As is often the case, our categories can obscure as much as they reveal. I certainly agree that Paul's letter is deeply theological. Yet Paul's language is not simply about *knowing* that God is creator or *assenting* to certain propositions about God. His language concerns rendering praise and thanksgiving, actions that are fundamentally actions of worship. Indeed, what Paul says in 1:18–32 is that humans in fact know of God but they refuse to worship God rightly.

That devastating critique of the human in Romans 1–3 and the restoration of worship in Romans 8 situate the large and complex challenge of describing the relationship between worship and ethics within the Christian life: What can we say about worship and ethics in a positive sense? What does genuine worship look like, ethically speaking? And what do ethics look like, viewed liturgically?

Answering those questions in a satisfying way would take us well beyond the limits of this volume, although I do have some initial observations that may be suggestive.

First, as I hope is obvious by now, claiming that worship occupies a significant role in this letter does not mean that Paul himself advocates a particular style of worship or offers hints about what elements do or do not belong in worship. He makes a single, slight reference to baptism (6:3–4), but there baptism is not the focus of attention. It provides us with an illustration rather than a directory of worship. First Corinthians is obviously a better letter for thinking about specific elements of worship, but even it is not going to solve contemporary worship wars for us.

Second, worship is enacted *in and through the letter itself*, as Paul anticipates or at least hopes that the letter will generate worship. In 1:25, for example, Paul recapitulates his complaint about the rebellion of human beings with the claim that "they exchanged the truth of God for a lie and they worshiped and served the creation rather than the creator." Then he continues with "the creator who is blessed forever, amen!" Following a clue from J. Louis Martyn, I have argued elsewhere[18] that Paul anticipates that, as the Roman Christians hear Phoebe reading the letter, they will join their own "Amen" to hers. "Amen," after all, has its native habitat in the context of worship.

Such expressions are scattered across the letter. Paul's difficult discussion about God's dealings with Israel both opens and closes with the word "Amen," as he invites the Roman audiences to praise God as they align themselves with his argument about God's mercy for Israel (indeed, for all people). Importantly, at the end of the letter body, after Paul has urged Roman Christians to pray for him, he closes with "the God of peace be with all of you. Amen" (15:33). In this way, he does not simply ask for prayer for his reception in Jerusalem. He (or his letter) actually sets that prayer in motion as the community gathers to hear his letter and his plea for their support.

18. Beverly Roberts Gaventa, "'For the Glory of God': Theology and Experience in Paul's Letter to the Romans," in *Between Experience and Interpretation: Engaging the Writings of the New Testament*, ed. Mary F. Foskett and O. Wesley Allen Jr. (Nashville: Abingdon, 2008), 53–65.

And he assumes that the gathered community will continue in prayer.

Paul hopes that the right relationship of worship and ethics will be generated by the reading of the letter, but he also hopes—expects, anticipates—that the relationship between worship and ethics will be enacted *within the community of those called into fellowship by God's action in the death and resurrection of Jesus Christ*. It may not be too much to say that the goal is to forge worship and ethics together in one "Amen."

One of the most obvious features of Romans 12:1–15:6, the "ethical" section of the letter, is its preoccupation with questions *internal* to community life. Reprising his comments in 1 Corinthians about the church as Christ's body, Paul writes, "Although we are many, we are one body in Christ, members of one another" (Rom. 12:5). That mutuality is reflected in much that follows, and it leads directly into Paul's treatment of the "strong" and the "weak" in Romans 14. The historical questions regarding this passage are numerous and complex, but it appears that there are some in Rome (both Jews and gentiles) who believe that the arrival of Jesus Christ as God's Messiah means that kosher laws have been set aside. For others in Rome (both Jews and gentiles), those laws remain in place. That disagreement has the potential to morph into conflict when the community gathers for common meals. If those who eat everything insist on putting everything on the serving table, then those who eat only what is kosher will be offended, possibly even scandalized.[19]

Paul's response is, predictably, theological. He argues that all Christians are household slaves of the same God, so no one has

19. Beverly Roberts Gaventa, "Reading for the Subject: The Paradox of Power in Romans 14:1–15:6," *JTI* 5 (2011): 1–12; John M. G. Barclay, "'Do We Undermine the Law?': A Study of Romans 14:1–15:6," in *Paul and the Mosaic Law*, ed. James D. G. Dunn, WUNT 89 (Tübingen: J. C. B. Mohr [Paul Siebeck], 1996), 287–308.

any business criticizing a fellow believer (14:1–12). He goes on, however, to ask that those who are comfortable eating everything compromise their privileges for the sake of those who may be led into bad faith by their example (14:13–23). Then comes the conclusion in 15:1–6:

> We who are [really] strong should bear with the weaknesses of those who are not strong and should not please ourselves. Let each of us please the neighbor for the good, for upbuilding, since Christ did not please himself. . . . And may the God of endurance and comfort grant you to think in the same way with one another, thinking according to Christ Jesus, *so that together with one mouth you might glorify the God and Father of our Lord Jesus Christ.*

The logic here is revealing: Paul offers instruction about dealing with difference, so that the community will come together (upbuilding). But that mutual respect and unity (not uniformity—unity) is not an end in itself. The goal, ultimately, is the glorification of God. Here the negative relationship between worship and behavior from 1:18–32 (i.e., the withholding of worship and the resultant malformed lives) is overcome in a community that together praises God.

The unity (not uniformity—unity) of the community in the praise of God might devolve into ecclesiastical self-preoccupation, such as appears in claims that the church exists only for the sake of the church, that it is not called to serve those outside its boundaries. In the following chapter I will have more to say about that issue, but for the present we may take note of Paul's discussion of the collection for Jerusalem in Romans 15.[20] While

---

20. The collection apparently was a major feature of Paul's mission. See 1 Cor. 16:1–4 and 2 Cor. 8–9; see also David Downs, *The Offering of the Gentiles: Paul's Collection for Jerusalem in Its Chronological, Cultural, and Cultic Contexts* (Grand Rapids: Eerdmans, 2016).

the beneficiaries are fellow Christians, they are apparently believers who are seriously at odds with Paul's understanding of the gospel, specifically of its inclusion of gentiles. Paul's impassioned request for prayer on behalf of this mission in 15:30–33 reveals the depth of his concern. To understand the anxiety, we might imagine some contemporary Christian group (for example, Christians deeply opposed to the practice of same-sex marriage) gathering funds to support a rival group (perhaps a group seeking same-sex marriage). Not only is Paul seeking to have the collection received, but he refers to it in liturgical terms. It is an offering (15:16) that the gentiles are making as an act of worship (15:28).[21]

If ethics is sustained and systematic reflection on moral conduct, then Paul does not have an ethic. As did the pastors who responded to Robin Scroggs's lecture, we want an ethic to tell us what to do and not do (and rather often we want one designed to tell other people what they should and should not do). And we may want to know what sort of people to be. But that is not what Paul is up to, at least not in the usual way. As with our previous chapters, we find that we have started at the wrong place. With questions of salvation, we start at the wrong place, as we do with questions about Israel. With ethics, we have started typically with specific questions, without inquiring after the underlying concerns.

In Romans, those underlying concerns have to do with the worship of God. Paul does not talk simply about having the right understanding of God. Instead, he talks about standing right before God, not just about thought but about worship.

---

21. The Greek is ambiguous, and scholars disagree about the translation. Some think Paul is referring to the gentiles themselves as the offering (as in Robert Jewett, *Romans: A Commentary*, Hermeneia [Minneapolis: Fortress, 2007], 907), but others think Paul is referring here to the offering the gentiles are making (as in Downs, *Offering of the Gentiles*, 147–57).

The arc of the letter, from 1:18 to 15:13, has to do with humanity rejecting the worship of God and, through the intervention of God in the gospel, being empowered to praise God in the company of others.

Donna Johnson's memoir, *Holy Ghost Girl*, recalls her early life spent on the sawdust trail.[22] Her mother was for years the organist for revivalist and faith healer David Terrell. The story is in some ways predictable, involving both sexual misconduct and fiscal mismanagement. Johnson herself was deeply hurt by Terrell's corruption, yet she describes wistfully the hours spent in the revival tent, the sense of transcendence, the power of gospel music, and the long periods given over to corporate prayer. She writes about the fact that in this tent, in Texas and across the Deep South in the 1950s and '60s, black and white people worshiped together. Together. At first, they sat in separate sections, which was already an affront to local culture and drew the attention of the Klan, but eventually Terrell insisted that they sit together. He would say, "We're all God's children, and we all sit together under my tent."[23] Johnson is painfully honest about the limitations of Terrell's practice, since both he and his circle continued blatantly racist practices outside the arena of worship.

While deeply disturbing, Johnson's memoir is also genuine testimony to the power of worship, even in lives as corrupted as our own. Of course, Paul is not speaking just about worship services, about formal liturgical acts. Yet I think Donna Johnson's depiction may bear confirming witness to the relationship Paul traces between worship and behavior. However troubling her account is of David Terrell's actions, he could not remain unchanged by worship, by his understanding that the

22. Donna Johnson, *Holy Ghost Girl* (New York: Gotham Books, 2012).
23. Ibid., 55.

tent—God's house—could not be a place for racial division. Even when the larger culture resisted and when his own shaping by that culture continued to grasp him by the throat, he could not entirely escape the voice of worship itself.

Inside the carapace of worship, even if nowhere else, we know who is our Lord, and we are shaped to live accordingly.

4

WHEN IN ROMANS . . .

WELCOME ONE ANOTHER

To understate matters considerably, anxiety about the future of the church permeates American Christianity in these early decades of the twenty-first century. The Pew Research Center only confirmed that anxiety when it released a study in May 2015 with the headline "Christians Decline Sharply as Share of Population; Unaffiliated and Other Faiths Continue to Grow."[1] That study intensified concerns among both clergy and laity, many of whom immediately set out to provide solutions in terms of new programs or strategies.

Romans will not supply us with specific programs or strategies for negotiating this perceived crisis. Romans can, however, instruct our understandings of the church. And once again,

---

1. Pew Research Center, "America's Changing Religious Landscape," May 12, 2015, http://www.pewforum.org/2015/05/12/americas-changing-religious-landscape/.

Romans may well challenge our constricted ways of thinking. As we will see, Paul's remarks suggest a clear, an empowered, even an exalted understanding of the gathered community at Rome. Yet the numerous admonitions in the letter reveal that Paul knows the church continues to be vulnerable to weaknesses of all sorts. He works to consolidate the church, especially across the lines of Jew and gentile.

For all his concern about building up the church's life, Paul is also concerned for the outside. The boundary around the community remains porous, subject to the actions of God rather than those of human beings. For the church to understand itself as existing in isolation, set apart *from* the world rather than *for* it, is a gross misreading of Paul's letters, as we will see below.

One of the small peculiarities of Romans is that Paul uses the word *ekklēsia* only in the final chapter of the letter.[2] Most of Paul's other letters begin by explicitly addressing the church or congregation, as in 1 Thessalonians 1:1:

Paul and Silas and Timothy to the church [*ekklēsia*] of the Thessalonians in God the Father and the Lord Jesus Christ . . .

Similar greetings appear in 1 Corinthians, 2 Corinthians, Galatians, and Philemon.[3] In Romans, however, the term *ekklēsia* appears neither in the opening salutation nor in the body of the letter but only in the greetings of chapter 16.[4] Even there,

2. Although *ekklēsia* is often translated "church," there is nothing peculiarly Christian about the term, which can be used for assemblies of several sorts. Here I use the translation "church" because one way of identifying Paul's view of the people who are later identified as the Christian church is by looking at his use of the term *ekklēsia*.
3. Phil. 1:1 addresses "all the holy ones in Christ Jesus who are in Philippi, together with the overseers and deacons." Yet the term *ekklēsia* does appear in 4:15 in reference to the Philippians (and see also Phil. 3:6).
4. Günter Klein has argued that the absence of the term *ekklēsia* in the body of Romans reflects Paul's view that there was, as yet, no real "church" at Rome because no apostle had founded it ("Paul's Purpose in Writing the Epistle to the Romans," in *The Romans Debate*, ed. Karl P. Donfried, 3rd ed. [Grand Rapids: Baker Academic,

"church" refers largely to groups outside Rome, as when Paul identifies Phoebe as a "deacon of the church in Cenchreae" (16:1) or writes that "all the churches of Christ greet you" (16:16). When he greets the various gatherings in Rome, Paul identifies only one as an *ekklēsia*, the one that meets in the home of Prisca and Aquila (16:5). As I mentioned in the introduction, however, the other greetings in chapter 16 may well each address separate gatherings of believers identified by their association with particular individuals. Although research continues on the meeting places of these gatherings, their size, and their constitution, what seems most obvious, at least at first glance, is that each group has a certain identity based on the identity of its hosts.[5] They each have clear boundaries and definitions, as we might expect. Each is the church or congregation that gathers in a particular place.

The Church Called into Faith

Paul does not specifically refer to the church, the *ekklēsia*, until chapter 16, and he does not appear to know the term "Christian,"[6] yet he often addresses a "you" (plural) or speaks

---

2011], 29–43). That particular argument has won few adherents, but my own view is that Paul regards the Romans as having a restricted understanding of the gospel, which he hopes to enlarge with this letter (see the introduction and ""To Preach the Gospel': Romans 1,15 and the Purposes of Romans," in *The Letter to the Romans*, ed. Udo Schnelle, BETL 226 [Leuven: Peeters, 2009], 179–95). That concern might explain the absence of the term in the salutation.

5. For discussion of Christian meeting places, see David Balch and Annette Weissenrieder, eds., *Contested Spaces: Houses and Temples in Roman Antiquity and the New Testament* (Tübingen: Mohr Siebeck, 2012); Edward Adams, *The Earliest Christian Meeting Places: Almost Exclusively Houses?* (London: T&T Clark/Bloomsbury, 2013).

6. "Christian" appears in the New Testament only in Acts 11:26 and 26:28 (as a slur by outsiders) and in 1 Pet. 4:16. On the names Christians employed for themselves, see Paul Trebilco, *Self-Designations and Group Identity in the New Testament* (Cambridge: Cambridge University Press, 2012).

alongside a "we"[7] that later generations would designate as Christians or as the church. The letter characterizes that group in several different ways, each of which reflects Paul's understanding of the gospel as well as the church that gospel has called into being.

The letter opens by addressing those who are "called to belong to Jesus Christ, everyone in Rome who is beloved of God, called to be holy" (1:6–7).[8] A shorthand reference for this address would be "those who believe," as in 1:16 and 3:22, or those who belong to Jesus-faith (3:26).[9] In an important passage at the end of chapter 4, Paul speaks of "us" as those who "trust in the one who raised Jesus our Lord from the dead, who was handed over because of our trespasses and raised for our righteousness" (4:24–25).

There is nothing especially surprising about these references to faith. As I indicated in the introduction, many know Romans primarily for its statements about faith, as in the following passages:

For I am not ashamed of the gospel, as it is God's own power bringing about salvation for everyone who believes, the Jew first and also the Greek. (1:16)

The rectification of God [has been made manifest] through Jesus Christ–faith for everyone who believes. (3:22)

7. To be sure, not every use of "we" in Romans reflects Paul's understanding of what it means to be the church. A number of instances of "we" are rhetorical formulations, as in the repeated use of the question "What shall we say?" (e.g., 4:1; 6:1; 7:7).
8. Paul is not the only one to speak of the "holiness" of believers, of course; see 1 Pet. 1:15–16. That usage has important precedents in Old Testament identifications of Israel as "holy," as in Deut. 7:6 and 14:2.
9. This statement reflects my position on the greatly disputed question of the "faith of Christ," a phrase that is usually translated either as "faith [or belief] in Christ" or as the "faith/faithfulness of Christ." Increasingly aware of the problems with both sides of the debate, I take the phrase to refer to God's action in Jesus Christ that returns to God as human trust in God. As shorthand for that event, I use "Christ-faith/Jesus-faith."

For everyone who calls on the Lord's name will be saved. (10:13; quoting Joel 3:5 LXX)

In addition, many people, both those within the church and those outside it, would identify Christians that way today, as those who believe in a certain way, conforming to a specific body of teaching. Paul's letters press us to nuance our understanding of faith, to put less stress on an intellectual decision or an individual action (as we saw in chap. 1). Still, it comes as no surprise to see Christians characterized as those who trust God, the one who "raised Jesus our Lord from the dead" (Rom. 4:24).

However important faith language may be in Romans, Paul speaks of "us" with a wealth of other language as well. "We" are also people who have peace with God, as 5:1 importantly states:

Therefore, since we have been rectified on the basis of faith, let us enjoy the peace we have before God through our Lord Jesus Christ.[10]

When the phrase "at peace with God" occurs in everyday speech, it often refers to being on God's "good side" or in good standing with God. Sometimes we hear it used of those who approach death with confidence in their relationship with God ("She's at peace with God"). Although Paul can and does speak confidently about his expectation of being "with Christ" after death (as in Phil. 1:21–24; see also 1 Thess. 4:17), the context in Romans suggests more is at stake for Paul than the salvation of the individual or even the salvation of the

---

10. There is a textual problem with the main verb in 5:1. Some ancient manuscripts read the present active indicative, "we have," while others read the present active subjunctive, "let us have," or as I have translated here, "let us enjoy." My point at present is simply that Paul assumes that "we" have peace with God.

church. As we saw in chapter 1 above, Paul employs conflict language frequently in Romans, and especially in chapters 5–8.[11] Being at peace with God means that "we" are no longer counted among God's enemies, as Paul indicates in 5:10 ("if when we were enemies . . ."). "We" have been reconciled to God (5:10). One characteristic of the Christian community, for Paul, is its understanding that God is in conflict with anti-God powers on behalf of all humanity. Christians, who were once God's enemies, now have their place as "weapons" in this battle:

> Do not present your members to Sin as weapons of wrong, but present your members to God as people alive from the dead,[12] and present your members to God as weapons of rectification. (6:13; see also 13:12)

Paul, then, thinks of Christians as those who know that there is a battle and who understand something about it. They have their place as "weapons" in God's battle, which means they endeavor to find their place in God's conflict. That endeavor comes to expression in texts such as Romans 15:30–32, when he urges the Roman Christians to "engage in battle along with me"[13] in prayer for his upcoming work in Jerusalem on behalf of the church's unity.

11. See also Beverly Roberts Gaventa, "The Rhetoric of Violence and the God of Peace in Paul's Letter to the Romans," in *Paul, John, and Apocalyptic Eschatology: Studies in Honour of Martinus C. de Boer*, ed. Jan Krans, B. J. Lietaert Peerbolte, Peter-Ben Smit, and Arie W. Zwiep, NovTSup (Leiden: Brill, 2013), 61–75.

12. This expression is difficult to translate into idiomatic English, since Paul compresses into three Greek words a larger notion that the gospel involves breathing life into people who were virtually dead.

13. The NRSV translates this request as "join me in earnest prayer to God on my behalf," which obscures the notion of conflict carried by the verb *synagōnizomai*. The NIV's "join me in my struggle" is an improvement, marginally, although "struggle" may be construed as a personal matter rather than something that takes place on a larger scale.

"We" are also characterized by life. Romans 5:17–18 introduces the notion that those who receive the gift of rectification receive "life," and 6:4 associates baptism with "newness of life" (and see again 6:13). By virtue of being baptized "into Christ Jesus," baptized into "his death" (6:3–4), "we" have new life that anticipates the resurrection itself (6:5). This new life empowers "us" to serve God rightly, because "we" have been liberated from the enslaving grasp of Sin and Death. Although he does not use the language of "new creation" here as he does elsewhere (2 Cor. 5:17; Gal. 6:15), Paul's argument in Romans is consistent with the notion that "we" are newly created and empowered for service by God's Spirit.

The notion of being empowered seems at odds with another of Paul's terms for believers, which is that "we" are slaves of God. He applies the term to himself in the opening line of the letter: he is a "slave of Christ" (Rom. 1:1). Christians, who were once enslaved to Sin, are now said to be slaves of righteousness, which is to say, slaves of God (6:16–18). Chapter 14 reflects this same view, since in that passage different (and conflicting) believers are analogized to servants in God's household.[14] Disconcerting as it is to contemporary readers, Paul does not operate with a notion of human freedom, if by that we mean being free to do whatever we please. Paul's view is better captured by Bob Dylan's lyric "You're gonna have to serve somebody."[15]

The shift from slavery to the power of Sin to slavery to God involves a shift of lordship, but it involves more than a change of ownership. At a crucial moment in Romans 8, Paul writes, "You did not receive a spirit of slavery again to fear, but you

14. Luke also uses the language of "slave" for Mary in Luke 1:38 and for Paul and Silas in Acts 16:17.
15. For the full lyrics to Dylan's "Gotta Serve Somebody," see http://www.bob dylan.com/us/songs/gotta-serve-somebody.

received a spirit of adoption by which we cry out" (8:15). Fear, of course, is part and parcel of slavery, which routinely subjects people to violence, threats of violence, and hence fear.[16] But here Paul changes keys, as it were. Being God's slave means that fear has been conquered, but it means far more than that: being God's slave is being part of the household, being "sons and daughters of God" (8:14). This is what God's slavery looks like; it looks like being adopted as a beloved child. Paul goes on to speak of "us" in even more extravagant terms, as those who are adopted by God, who are able to call God "Father," who are heirs along with Christ, who are even glorified with Christ as their "brother" (8:16–17).

Such extravagant notions are tempered, however. The "we" who are glorified with Christ also suffer along with him (8:17).[17] In 8:18–27 Paul speaks movingly about the expectation of all creation for redemption, an expectation that includes the "we" of believers. "We" have received the first fruit; "we" have the Spirit as intercessor. The assumption here is that "we" are under attack but also that God will do battle on "our" behalf. And "we" will be "supervictors" (8:37; and see 5:17).[18]

Given the expansive character of the gospel Paul preaches, the diverse imagery he uses to speak about its impact on human life should come as no surprise. This array of language places us at considerable distance from the notion that Christians are simply those who believe a certain way, who conform to a particular set of doctrines. The language encompasses virtually the whole of human life and cannot be restricted to assent to a few propositions.

16. See especially Orlando Patterson, *Slavery and Social Death: A Comparative Study* (Cambridge, MA: Harvard University Press, 1982).

17. See Ann Jervis, *At the Heart of the Gospel: Suffering in the Earliest Christian Message* (Grand Rapids: Eerdmans, 2007).

18. The vivid translation "supervictors" is that of Robert Jewett, *Romans: A Commentary*, Hermeneia (Minneapolis: Fortress, 2007), 548.

"One Body in Christ"

The rich variety of language for Christians we have just sur-
veyed works itself out in Romans 12–15, where Paul addresses
specific challenges to Christian life, especially Christian life in
community. He opens with a clear statement about Christians
belonging to one another in Christ:

> Just as in one body we have many members, and all the mem-
> bers do not have the same use, thus although we are many,
> we are one body in Christ, and members each one of others.
> (12:4–5)

The language of being "in Christ" has already appeared in
two of Paul's letters. In Galatians 3:28 it serves to demar-
cate the single place in which believers exist, their singular
identity in Christ despite gender, ethnicity, or social status.
In 1 Corinthians 12 it introduces an argument about how differences in spiritual gifts should not be grounds for envy but
should rather contribute to the unity of the body of Christ
in worship.

In the immediate context of Romans 12, Paul does several
things on the basis of this image. To begin with, he deduces
from the imagery of the body of Christ the notion that we have
responsibilities to and for one another. Being members of one
another means that there is a relationship from which there
is no exit plan. Having been brought together, Christians do
not have the option of walking away from one another. That
in itself challenges a great deal in contemporary church life,
both positively and negatively. Negatively, the notion that we
have responsibilities to and for one another is in open conflict
with the dominant Western idolatry of the individual, which
allows us to imagine that we are free from the needs and claims
of others.

Positively, as Paul develops his argument, he encourages Roman Christians to contribute to the whole through the spiritual gifts they have received. Already he has said that God has measured out faith (12:3), and here he takes up gifts, however briefly. Prophecy, ministry, teaching, exhorting, giving, leading, showing compassion: all these gifts are to be lived out to the fullest capacity of the recipient.

It is worth noting that twice in this context Paul expresses concern about those who think too highly of their own opinions:

> Do not think beyond what you ought to think but think in a sober fashion. (12:3)

> Do not think arrogant thoughts but associate with the modest.[19] Don't be wise among yourselves. (12:16)

These comments betray concern about those who trample over the convictions of others (as in chap. 14; see below). These admonitions to modesty about one's own judgments do not require that believers become "doormats for the Lord," much less "doormats for one another," as one student long ago told me she had been taught. The concern may well reflect the situation at Rome or elsewhere.

We often hear these admonitions in worship or encounter them in Christian literature—so often that they become little more than elevator music, predictable pronouncements that seldom make their way into our consciousness. We take them as bland encouragements to get along with one another, to "make nice." But their demand becomes clear when the church is tested by conflict. What happens then? That question brings us to Romans 14.

---

19. This phrase is ambiguous and can refer either to modest thoughts or to those of modest situation.

"Welcome One Another"

> Welcome the one who is weak in faith, but not s
> putes about opinions. On one side is the one wh
> eat anything, and on the other side the weak pei
> vegetables. (14:1–2)

This perplexing admonition plunges us into some sort of church dispute.[20] What exactly has happened to produce this dispute (or what Paul thinks has happened) may have been obvious to Phoebe's first auditors, but we are left to piece together the situation with only slivers of information. Here I offer one possible scenario, while acknowledging that scholarly opinion is significantly divided.[21] And I offer the scenario in rather bold strokes in order to highlight the importance of this conflict and Paul's response to it.

As noted earlier, "the church at Rome" probably consisted of several small groups of people who met in residences. Whether these were larger homes or crowded tenement dwellings or some other venue is disputed.[22] The important point for the moment is that there were several of them. Each of these gatherings had its own character; they varied not only in leadership but possibly even in their interpretations of the message about Jesus of Nazareth. They did not often come together across group lines, as it simply was not practical. When they did gather across group lines, as when they met as individual congregations, there was a shared meal.

20. Although some scholars contend that Paul is here addressing a generalized or hypothetical situation, many agree that he is aware of a particular issue at Rome.

21. For a survey of some major positions in this debate, see Mark Reasoner, *The Strong and the Weak: Romans 14:1–15:13 in Context*, SNTSMS 103 (Cambridge: Cambridge University Press, 1999), 1–23.

22. See Jewett, *Romans*, 53–55, 62–70, and the literature cited there. See also the recent work of Adams, *Earliest Christian Meeting Places*, who argues that they may have met in settings other than domestic.

The shared meal is apparently where the trouble started. Some people, those whom Paul identifies as the "weak in faith," insist on observing Mosaic food laws themselves, and they share table fellowship only with others who also observe the food laws. Although it seems obvious that some of these "weak in faith" would be Jews for whom the food laws are customary, it is likely also that some are gentiles who identify with Jews and their traditions.[23] In 14:2 Paul says that these people "eat only vegetables," which could reflect their extreme concern about avoiding unclean food, but it could also be a sort of slur: "These folks are so 'pure' that they eat only lettuce."

Other people, as Paul puts it in 14:2, "have faith to eat everything." We customarily speak of these people as "the strong," but it is important to see that Paul does not speak of them as strong. He only refers to "the strong" when he arrives at 15:1, and even then he may be using irony (as in "we who are *really* strong"). These are what he calls "faith-havers" (in 14:2), people who do not regard themselves as obliged to observe the food laws. They also do not observe the Sabbath, but the main conflict concerns food, as is clear from the discussion that follows. They eat everything; to others they will appear to be something like "garbage-bellies," people whose appetites are out of control. Paul is throwing an elbow in each direction: he elbows those who are squeamish by calling them "weak" in faith ("lettuce-eaters"), but he also takes a jab at those who eat anything ("garbage-bellies").

Everyone gets along just fine, so long as everyone is eating in isolation or in small groups of the like-minded. (Parallels to contemporary groups that occupy their own comfortable places in social media are painfully obvious.) Friction begins

23. Peter Lampe, *From Paul to Valentinus: Christians at Rome in the First Two Centuries*, trans. Michael Steinhauser, ed. Marshall D. Johnson (Minneapolis: Fortress, 2003), 69–79.

when they gather across these group lines for a shared meal. To cast the situation in contemporary terms: if the dinner is at my house, and I insist on serving only Tofu Surprise and ban pork barbecue from the table, then we could be in for a rough evening. That way of putting the dilemma is vivid, but it also severely understates the problem. Food laws were not about individual dietary decisions; they had to do with nothing less than Jewish identity. The resulting conflict about food could impede any unified gathering, and without a unified gathering, is there a church at Rome?

Paul's response reveals a great deal about his understanding of the church.[24] In the first half of the chapter (14:1–12), he takes this dispute and places it squarely in the context of the gospel. With three assertions about God and Christ, he undercuts any assumption that human beings have the right to sit in judgment of others:

- God is the householder, the only one who supervises every member of the household, and therefore the only one with the authority to judge human behavior (v. 4).
- Christ, by virtue of the resurrection, is the ruler over both the dead and the living, so that "we" belong to him and not to ourselves (vv. 7–9).
- Because all people will finally stand before God, only God is judge (vv. 10–11).

Nothing here should surprise anyone who has read the letter from the beginning (or heard it read, as its first audiences did). The early chapters of the letter identify humanity as having a single underlying problem that takes a variety of forms—namely,

24. Here I am drawing on an earlier discussion of this passage in Beverly Roberts Gaventa, "Reading for the Subject: The Paradox of Power in Romans 14:1–15:6," *JTI* 5 (2011): 1–12.

the refusal to acknowledge God as God (cf. 1:18–32). If human life belongs not to itself but to the God who has liberated it from captivity to Sin and Death, then it follows that human beings have no authority to judge one another. For Paul, judgment belongs to God alone.

Similarly, when Paul writes that Christ reigns as Lord of the living and of the dead (14:9), we may hear echoes of Romans 5, which talks about Grace ruling as king (5:21), a rule that triumphed over the twin powers of Sin and Death. And when he writes in 14:4 that God is "able to make that one stand," we hear the powerful assurance from the end of chapter 8: no power that exists has the power to separate "us" from the love of God in Christ Jesus, because God has the power to preserve "us." God's power to preserve "us" means that human judgment is irrelevant at best, arrogant and wrongheaded at worst.

These claims about divine power fund Paul's instructions about not judging one another, but they also set up the second half of the chapter (14:13–23). Here, the gears shift. The first half of the chapter is remarkably evenhanded, with parallel instructions to the "lettuce-eaters" and the "garbage-bellies." The instructions and warnings in verses 13–23 speak largely to the "garbage-bellies," however. There are, to be sure, some individual statements that pertain to both sides, such as the admonition to "pursue peace and upbuilding" (v. 19). But for the most part, Paul is concerned here with those who may stock the common table with foods that would offend and create a crisis of conscience for others.

The argument shows the "garbage-bellies" that they have a great deal of power and urges them to use it with care. Paul agrees with their position that food is neither clean nor unclean (see v. 14), and yet they should beware of putting "a stumbling block or a scandal" before a fellow Christian (v. 13). Verses 20–21 again use the language of stumbling block:

Everything is clean, but it is evil to the one who eat
of a stumbling block. It is good not to eat meat
drink wine, and not to do anything else by which y
or sister falls.

The language escalates with the contention that the "garbage-
bellies" actually have power sufficient to destroy others:

So if through food your sister is grieved, you are no longer living in accord with love. Do not through your food destroy that
one for whom Christ died. (14:15)

Do not, because of food, destroy God's work. (14:20a)

Over against the claims about God's saving power in the first
half of the chapter, these warnings about the misuse of human
power are of special concern.

Paul is still not finished with this depiction of the "garbage-
bellies," however. Alongside this destructive potential, they also
are able to pursue "peace" and "upbuilding" (v. 19). They do
this when they recognize that God's kingdom is not made up
of food and drink (v. 17), that God's own powerful rule does
not exist simply for the exercise of their own freedom.

Paul concludes this argument with 15:1–6, where he does
finally introduce direct reference to "the strong." Yet the actions of the ones Paul *now* designates as powerful (as genuinely
powerful) are not actions of eating and drinking to the down-
fall of others. They are instead those of setting aside one's
own convictions for the upbuilding of the neighbor. They are
learned, not from exercising the faith to eat anything, but from
the death of Christ, who did not "please himself" (15:3). And
the result of this exercise of genuine power is not mere tolerance
or human community as a good in and of itself. The result is
nothing less than the unified praise of God's saving glory (15:6).

111

In some sense, the specific problem Paul addresses in this passage is what we would label "practical": What are we to do in a particular situation when there is a dispute about a specific question of church practice? Importantly, Paul addresses problems related to what we call "church practice," but he thinks about them theologically. That may seem an obvious response, but it is not at all obvious in the way we customarily proceed.

Consider the particular issue of Romans 14 and translate it, however feebly, into the present: the problem concerns the church supper, specifically, what dishes belong on the table. Do the vegans run the house, because including even Tuna Surprise will compromise their deeply held principles? Or do the omnivores triumph with their rule that anything goes? Admittedly, as I noted above, much more was attached to the dietary question than would be in our context, but it is worth considering how it would be addressed in our congregations.

My hunch is that most of us would think in terms of solving the problem at hand. We would institute two different serving lines, one for the vegans, one for the omnivores. Keep the groups separate from each other during the meal; if necessary, use two dining areas and then bring everyone together for worship or study afterward.[25] For Paul, however, this practical challenge cannot be addressed apart from prior theological convictions. What funds Paul's response is the story of God's action of redeeming a captive humanity from the powers of Sin and Death, a story of God's re-creation of humanity for unity and thanksgiving, a story that has run throughout this letter. The divide between theology and practice that we take for granted does not exist for Paul.

As a result, when he confronts what might at first glance seem to be a "merely" practical problem, he thinks about it

---

25. The analogy breaks down quickly, since separating the meal from worship or study would probably be alien to the Roman congregations.

theologically, addressing the theological problem that is at stake before turning to the embodiment of that problem in the community's life.

The Way "We" Live Now:[26] The Church in Romans

This chapter has examined Paul's language for "us" and discussions about "us" for his understanding of the church. Now I want to look for the larger convictions about the church at work in this letter, while recognizing that Paul's is one voice in a much larger canonical conversation that has implications for the life of the church. It is also important to acknowledge at the outset that the church is not and cannot be a static entity. It was not static in the first century, with expressions in Jerusalem that differed significantly from those in Thessalonica and in Rome. What we look for when we ask about any biblical text and the life of the contemporary church has less to do with finding a template to be duplicated than with hearing witnesses to God's work in every age that shape us as we seek to bear witness together in our own time.

Crucial to understanding Paul's comments about "us," as we have seen, is that *the church is God's*. It belongs to God as the one who both called it into being (called "us" to faith) and sustains it. It is not a voluntary association, composed of those who have decided to affiliate with others for self-improvement or like belief or fellowship or even service, but a gathering of all those "called to be holy" (1:7).

It is because of God's activity, especially activity through the Spirit, that Paul can speak of "us" in the exalted language of Romans 8. Those who are "led by God's spirit" (8:14) are

---

26. With apologies to Anthony Trollope for playing on the title of his excellent novel.

identified as God's "children," as "heirs," as "fellow heirs with Christ" (vv. 16–17). A few lines later, Paul speaks of those who have been called as having been identified in advance, as brothers and sisters of Jesus Christ, as called, rectified, even glorified (vv. 29–30).

And yet. And yet. *This soaring language does not isolate "us" from problems, either external or internal.* That is clear already in Romans 8, since this soaring language about the glorification of "us" is housed within a larger acknowledgment that "we" experience suffering (8:17), that "we" groan in the present time (v. 23), and that there are powers that continue to undertake to remove "us" from the rule of God through Jesus Christ (vv. 31–39). The language of 8:31 reveals Paul's assumption: "If God is for us, who is against us?" No power will be able to stand "against us" finally. Apart from the list in 8:35, Paul does not specify the situations he has in mind, but the admonitions about dealing with opposition in 12:18–21 *may* suggest his concerns about external resistance.

Whatever external resistance there may be, Paul is at times clear that there are problems within the community. In addition to the conflict generated by the sharing of meals, there appears to be a larger problem arising from those who want to restrict God's actions in Jesus Christ to themselves and others who think as they do. Paul makes a general observation about this problem in 12:16 when he argues against holding too high a view of one's own opinions, but it has already emerged with some specificity in Romans 11. Having already insisted that God has not "rejected God's people" (11:1) and explained that the current division in Israel comes about as God's own action, Paul turns to address gentiles directly: "I am speaking to you gentiles" (11:13).

He then interprets his own ministry in the context of Israel's current division, and he interprets the gentile mission through the analogy of gentiles being grafted onto the olive tree, before he insists quite bluntly: "Do not boast over the branches. For if you boast, you do not carry the root, but the root carries you" (11:18). It appears that Paul knows (or at least suspects) that some gentiles among the "we" understand themselves to have displaced Jews. Although elements in this passage remain perplexing, the prohibition against arrogance toward others (whether Christian or not) is adamant. The prohibition has been prepared for by the emphasis throughout the letter on God's action for both Jew and gentile.

Gentile arrogance may not be the only difficulty. Paul also seems to be aware that some Jewish Christians reject the universal implications of the gospel. His urgent request that Roman Christians pray for his upcoming trip to Jerusalem is more than a hope for a smooth journey with few inconveniences. Paul fears that his ministry, perhaps especially the offering collected from his gentile churches for Jewish Christians (11:25–26), may be rejected precisely because the offering reflects the universal horizon of the gospel (11:30–33).

These challenges to the church's life are familiar territory to early twenty-first-century Christians. Paul's concern for the interior of the community—for its upbuilding, its solidarity—is an attractive position in our time, when the church (in many of its forms) finds itself so beleaguered that we are drawn to those elements of Scripture that allow us to draw the boundary of the community with bold colors. *That makes it all the more important to see that these challenges to the community—both from outside and from inside—prompt Paul to seek upbuilding, but they do not prompt him to anxious monitoring of the community's border.*

In our own time, when the church feels itself beleaguered, it is easy to respond by monitoring the boundaries for aberrant thought or behavior. Yet Paul does not seem particularly concerned about drawing a clear boundary marker around the church. The issue of observing or not observing *kashrut*, which to many would have been a community-dividing issue, was not such for Paul. Elsewhere, of course, Paul does draw lines. In 1 Corinthians, the man who is sleeping with his father's wife is to be expelled (5:1–5). The Galatians are urged to drive out the Jewish Christian teachers (4:30). But here in Romans, Paul is content to affirm that God is the owner of the household, that God is the one who calls the community into being; by implication, any disputes about its membership are settled by God.

Paul is by no means indifferent to questions of Christian identity. In Romans 6 he draws a sharp line when he refers to the difference made by baptism into Christ. And in chapter 8 he distinguishes between living in the realm of the flesh and living in the realm of the Spirit. Believers know what time it is: "Our salvation is nearer than when we began to believe" (13:11). Believers are, according to Romans 12, "one body in Christ, and members one of another" (v. 5).

So the Christian community has boundaries, but boundaries can often be misleading. While Paul clearly wants to strengthen the connections within the congregation (I think especially of 1 Thessalonians and 1 Corinthians), he does not do that by demonizing outsiders. Second Peter 2 disparages false teachers, and 1 John castigates "children of the devil" (3:8). In the Dead Sea Scrolls, the "Rule of the Community" instructs members of the community to "hate all the Children of Darkness, each commensurate with his guilt and the vengeance due him from God" (1QS 1.10–11). Little in Paul's letters approaches that level of vitriol.

To the contrary, in Romans Paul demonstrates a remarkable concern for the outsider. At the end of Romans 12, he urges peacemaking, not taking revenge on the persecutor, doing good to all people. This is quite an impressive element in Paul's thought. He might well have been tempted to pull up the draw-bridge, to argue for a community that cares only for itself and castigates those on the outside. Paul seldom indulges in that temptation, and his stance is reflective of his understanding that God has acted in Christ Jesus for all human beings, both for those who are called to see that action in the present and for those who live unaware of God's grace. The community of those grasped by the God who raised Jesus from the dead does not reside in gated enclaves of the smug and condescending.

CONCLUSION

The song known as "This Train" or "This Train Is Bound for Glory" would find a place on any list of best-known American folk songs. Some of us learned it by means of Woody Guthrie and may have thought he wrote it, but its origins are actually unknown.[1] First recorded in the 1920s, "This Train" became a hit in the 1930s as sung by Sister Rosetta Tharpe. Since then it has been recorded by a number of performers. The most famous rendition may be that of Peter, Paul, and Mary, but the dizzying array of recordings includes Louis Armstrong, Jimmy Durante, Bob Marley, Joni Mitchell, Johnny Cash, Mahalia Jackson, the Staples Singers, and Mumford and Sons.[2]

The lyrics vary with the vocalists, but two things remain constant. First, there are folks who qualify to ride on "this train"—the righteous and the holy. Second, there are people

1. Among the reasons for associating the song with Guthrie is that it features prominently in his autobiographical *Bound for Glory* (New York: E. P. Dutton, 1976).

2. To my knowledge, the earliest published version of the lyrics for "This Train" appears in John A. Lomax and Alan Lomax, *American Ballads and Folk Songs* (New York: Macmillan, 1935), 593–94. On "This Train" and other religious songs involving railways, see Norm Cohen, *Long Steel Rail: The Railroad in American Folksong* (Urbana: University of Illinois Press, 2000), 596–644.

who will not be allowed to board the train. Big Bill Broonzy's early version stipulates that there is "no Jim Crow and no discrimination" on this train. Mahalia Jackson's rendition outlaws tobacco chewers and cigar smokers. Woody Guthrie's well-known version excludes a long list of misbehavers, including gamblers, side-street walkers, and two-bit hustlers. The cast of characters barred from travel changes somewhat from one version to another, as various performers modify their list of what counts as unrighteousness. But in all of them, you have to be holy to get on board.

Against this durable understanding of the train "bound for glory," Bruce Springsteen's "Land of Hope and Dreams" is more than a little off-key.[3] The melody differs from that of "This Train," but the genetic relationship to the earlier train song is unmistakable. Yet here the logic of the earlier song is overturned. In Springsteen's version, the train carries "saints and sinners," and Springsteen itemizes those "saints and sinners" in gleeful detail.[4] In the world invoked by the Boss's song, the train requires no ticket, no proof of suitability.

There is no mistaking Springsteen's intention here, since he explicitly reported that he wanted to make his song inclusive of all people.[5] In an interview, Springsteen also reported why he chose to include "Land of Hope and Dreams" on his *Wrecking Ball* album. He wanted a "really big song," something with "size" and a "spiritual" dimension that would complete the

3. Written in 1998, the song was performed in concert and included in performance albums but not recorded in a studio until Springsteen's *Wrecking Ball* album in 2012.

4. The full lyrics may be found at http://brucespringsteen.net/albums/wreckingball. Rob Kirkpatrick aptly describes Springsteen's song as "an all-inclusive joyride with universal invites" (in *The Words and Music of Bruce Springsteen* [Westport, CT: Praeger, 2007], 141). In that sense, it also diverges from Curtis Mayfield's "People Get Ready," elements of which are included in the final lines of "Land of Hope and Dreams."

5. Bruce Springsteen, *Bruce Springsteen: Songs* (San Francisco: Harper Entertainment, 2001), 296.

narrative arc opened up by the social outrage that characterizes the early songs in the album, such as "Easy Money" and "We Take Care of Our Own."[6] Listening to Springsteen's version, it is easy to imagine a long line of his predecessors, extending all the way back to and beyond Sister Rosetta Tharpe, listening and scratching their heads in amazement: How did *those* people get a place on *my* train?

Confronting the "All" of Romans

Bruce Springsteen may never have read Paul's Letter to the Romans, but the "all" that underlies "Land of Hope and Dreams" nevertheless echoes the stunning "all" of Paul's most influential letter. As we have seen repeatedly in this study, God's action is for "all." Most famously, the theme of the letter announces the "all":

> I am not ashamed of the gospel, for it is God's own power bringing about salvation for everyone who believes, first the Jew and then the Greek. (1:16)

The "everyone" here is *pas* in Greek (like "*pan*demonium" or "*pan*demic"), translated "all" in some places and "every" in others. Paul uses the little word "all" quite frequently in this letter. Sometimes "all" concerns the universal extent of sin, as in 3:9: "All, both Jews and Greeks, are under the power of Sin." Paul reiterates that point in 3:19–20 with the claim that the law closes every (*pas*) mouth and that the whole (*pas*) world is under judgment. No one is rectified on the basis of observance of the law (literally, "all flesh is not . . .").

---

6. These comments come from a press conference held in Paris, February 2012; see *Talk about a Dream: The Essential Interviews of Bruce Springsteen*, ed. Christopher Phillips and Louis P. Masur (New York: Bloomsbury, 2013), 409–10.

The action of God in the gospel of Jesus Christ renders this "all" of condemnation an "all" of redemption. In Romans 3, when Paul announces what he means about God's righteous act in the death of Jesus, he writes that, just as "all have sinned," "all" are also freely made right by God's grace through faith (3:22). Even the stipulation of faith slips away when Paul expands on his understanding of the gospel in the second half of Romans 5. The basis of the contrast between Adam and Christ is that each of them acted, and each action carried along with it the whole of humankind: just as one man's trespass led to condemnation for all, so one man's act of righteousness leads to justification and life for all (5:18).

The winding argument of Romans 9–11 regarding God's relationship to Israel culminates with the expectation that "all Israel will be saved" (11:26) and that "God has confined all in disobedience so that God might have mercy on all" (11:32).

But it isn't only these specific references that are telling. Romans 8 anticipates God's redemption of the entirety of creation with its language about creation groaning in expectation (vv. 18–25). And Romans 15:7–13 anticipates the doxology of Jew and gentile together in response to God's action in Jesus Christ. This "all" recalls the famous passage in Philippians 2, in which Paul summarizes the whole of the gospel story, culminating with the promise that

> at the name of Jesus
>   every knee should bend,
>   in heaven and on earth and under the earth,
>   and every tongue should confess
>   that Jesus Christ is Lord,
>   to the glory of God the Father. (Phil. 2:10–11 NRSV)

Simply put, the gospel claims the totality of creation. When "knees bend" in every place Paul can imagine, they bend to acknowledge ("every tongue . . . confess") the lordship of Jesus Christ.

In these passages, Paul is very far from imagining the gospel as a kind of offer God makes to individuals who are burdened by their own sins. As we saw in our discussion of salvation in chapter 1, it is simply larger than we imagine, both by virtue of the problem addressed and by virtue of God's all-encompassing action. A similar dynamic surfaced in the discussion of Israel in chapter 2, where we found that Paul's argument is that God created Israel and will sustain Israel, the whole of Israel, however peculiar human beings may find God's way of doing things.

This "all" extended also into the chapters on ethics (worship [chap. 3]) and the church (chap. 4). And we may not overlook that. By reaching out to include all, God also claims all—that is, the whole of human life. That is why Paul can say something very close to "Throw your bodies in the offering plate." It is also why he can nurture the life of the community, encouraging it in mutual support and upbuilding, while always at the very same time seeking the good of those on the outside.

This is scarcely the place to argue the exact contours of Paul's "all," and I do not wish to claim too much certainty for my argument, particularly given the ending of Romans 11, with its insistence that no one knows the mind of God:

> O the depth of the riches and wisdom and knowledge of God! How unsearchable are his judgments and how inscrutable his ways! (11:33 NRSV)

Yet I am inclined to hear Romans as an elaboration of the conclusion of the Philippians hymn—"Every knee will bow and every tongue will confess that Jesus Christ is Lord"—and to think that "all" indeed means all. As paraphrased by Springsteen, "You don't need no ticket. You just get on board."

But What about . . . ?

Challenging questions immediately crowd into our heads following any such conclusion. Below I offer a few brief reflections on them, but I do so with the clear recognition that I am *one* reader of Romans. In no way do I imagine myself speaking for the whole canon of Scripture, to say nothing of presuming to speak for God.

First, what does this "all," this universal horizon, imply about faith? Don't people have to believe in order to be accepted by God? After all, Romans 1:16 says that salvation is for "everyone who believes," and faith is undoubtedly an important element in the letter.

When thinking about that faith language, we need to recall that, for Paul, faith itself is a gift. In 12:3 he writes of God dealing out "a measure of faith" to each. The gift-character of faith is implicit in his language about believers being "called" (as in Rom. 1:6–7; 8:30; 1 Cor. 1:9; Gal. 1:6; 5:8; 1 Thess. 2:12), and it is explicit in passages such as Philippians 1:29: "You have received the gift as it concerns Christ, not only to believe in him but even to suffer for him." The fact that the gift is given to some people in the present does not limit God's capacity to bestow that gift on others—even on all people.

Especially for North American Christians, the notion of faith as a decision, a free human response, is so hardwired that it is difficult to understand the problems such a view carries with it. What is to be said of the individual with a profound intellectual disability, who simply cannot in any recognizable way come to a decision for or against belief in God? Of course, we can attribute to God a kind of exemption system for such people, or we can impute to them some hidden relationship to God that God regards as faith. By doing that, however, we are implicitly constructing a second class of human beings around such distinctions. We presume that such individuals are really not people at all (which is how they are sometimes treated). My point is not to address this vast question here but instead to underscore the difficulties of imagining that our response to God is a matter of individual belief or unbelief.[7]

A second and perhaps even more difficult question is, what does this universal horizon mean about really bad people? Does God's universal welcome extend to them as well? Does Romans suggest that there is salvation even for Adolf Hitler, to take the most notorious example available to us?[8] Aren't there some gradations among human beings, some distinctions between the good and the bad? This is a deeply disturbing question, as of course it is meant to be. And once again we need to recall the end of Romans 11 and remember that we do not have the mind of God.

The problem with such questions, at least from the point of view of Romans, is that they bring back in the very distinction Paul works so hard to expel—namely, the distinction between "good" people and "bad" people. Recall once again the relentless way in which Paul contends that all human beings are under Sin's power (see chap. 1 above). Questions about "bad" people presuppose that we, the question-posers, know who stands on each side of the line, that we know who gets to board the train. Paul does not need to show the difficulty of salvation for history's monsters; it is hard enough to show salvation for those we deem to be "good."

It may be that we need to introduce a different sort of question here, one less preoccupied with discovering God's attitude to others than with acknowledging our own anxious need to

---

7. I have reflected on this question also in "Which Humans? What Response? A Reflection on Pauline Theology," *ExAud* 30 (2014): 50–64.

8. See the remarks on this point by Stanley Stowers in *A Rereading of Romans: Justice, Jews, and Gentiles* (New Haven: Yale University Press, 1994), 176.

separate ourselves from those "other" people. That very desire all too often leaves us both blind to our own faults and susceptible to the very evils we would anathematize elsewhere.[9]

Third, if Paul does have this universal horizon, then what is the impetus to his mission? Would Paul have devoted himself to intense mission across the Mediterranean world had he not believed that individual faith and behavior were important, even salvifically important? Why the lament at the beginning of Romans 9, if Paul did not fear the failure of Christian mission?

Admittedly, he does say in Romans 11:14 that he hopes to save "some" of his kinfolk, which might suggest that he anticipated a time when "some" would be saved and others would not be. Yet, when Paul comments on his motive for preaching and teaching, he says that he has been *sent* to do that work. But that is far from the end of his argument, which culminates in the claim that "all" Israel will be saved (11:26). On the whole, when Paul speaks of his labor, he speaks about it as a task assigned him by God for God's own reasons. He is a "slave of Christ" (Rom. 1:1; Gal. 1:10; Phil. 1:1). He is called to this work (Rom. 1:1; 1 Cor. 1:1; 15:9; Gal. 1:15), set apart from before his birth (Gal. 1:15). His sense of compulsion is such that he can announce, "Woe to me if I do not proclaim the gospel!" (1 Cor. 9:16 NRSV; and see 1 Cor. 9:17; Gal. 2:7; 1 Thess. 2:4).

More to the point, Paul proclaims the gospel because he believes it to be true, because it is indeed good news (i.e., gospel), and because that good news brings with it comfort and encouragement and hope. Paul's earliest letter may help us at just this point, since he opens by giving thanks for the way the

9. Matt. 7:1–6 comes to mind, as well as Flannery O'Connor's story "Revelation," in *Everything That Rises Must Converge* (New York: Farrar, Straus & Giroux, 1956), 191–218. See also J. Louis Martyn's "From Paul to Flannery O'Connor with the Power of Grace," in *Theological Issues in the Letters of Paul* (Nashville: Abingdon, 1997), 279–97.

Thessalonians flourished under the gift of the gospel. He goes on to say of himself and his coworkers, "You know what kind of persons we proved to be among you for your sake" (1 Thess. 1:5 NRSV). He then comments on the joy present at Thessalonica, introducing a dimension of the gospel all too often neglected in our discussions. The act of God in Jesus Christ produces joy (see especially Rom. 14:17; 15:13; 2 Cor. 1:24; 2:3; 7:13; Gal. 5:22). Why would one *not* tell that news? That joy in turn may explain Paul's lament in Romans 9:1–5 over his relatives who do not yet share in God's inexpressible gift.

A related and final question is, where is the ethical imperative in this universal horizon? Where is the incentive to behave? What good is the gospel if people don't behave better? I would answer that question similarly to the one above. In the gospel, God does not simply instruct and exhort. God releases humanity from its inability and, indeed, re-creates humanity (2 Cor. 5:17; Gal. 6:15). This new creation is able to hear an admonition as people who have received an empowering gift (Rom. 12:1–2). Paul is fully aware that even this new creation is only the very beginning of what God will accomplish (Rom. 8:18–25). The numerous problems he addresses in his letters reveal that Christians are very much capable of sinning, but the admonitions also carry with them the promise that God will not leave humanity to itself (as in Rom. 15:6, 13; 8:31–39).

These comments will likely provoke sharp dissent. Again I want to insist that I raise this question of the universal horizon of Romans not because I have an answer for it in just a few paragraphs. It is not at all clear that Paul was consciously addressing that question in Romans or elsewhere. Nor would I claim, even if I were certain I understood *Paul's* answer, that his answer is shared by other biblical witnesses. My reason for pressing this question is once again to put before us the vastness of the gospel. What we need to hear is that the gospel encompasses the cosmos, the whole of creation—all the way out and all the way down in each of us.

The first time I taught Paul's Letter to the Romans, I began by making a simple assignment. I asked the class, a group of seminary students, to read the letter from beginning to end in one sitting. They were to do that before looking at any textbook or commentary.

Before the class met, a student came to me, quite distraught. She said, barely able to control her voice, "I just cannot do this assignment. I cannot read Romans." As we talked, the reasons came tumbling out. The voice she heard when she read Romans was a fairly stilted, artificially liturgical voice, droning out the letter. Line after line washed over her, lulling her into inattention. She simply could not stay with it. She could not hold on long enough to make sense of the argument, so lifeless had the letter become to her.

I hope this volume will prove useful to those who have had similar experiences. I hope a real letter will come into view now, one over which we will linger. Beyond that, I hope that we catch a glimpse of God's vast love and longing and determination for all of us. I hope that, with Springsteen, we imagine a train capacious enough to hold us all.

FOR FURTHER READING

General Introductions to Paul and His Letters

Bassler, Jouette. *Navigating Paul: An Introduction to Key Theological Concepts*. Louisville: Westminster John Knox, 2007.

Cousar, Charles B. *The Letters of Paul*. Interpreting Biblical Texts. Nashville: Abingdon, 1996.

Gray, Patrick. *Opening Paul's Letters: A Reader's Guide to Genre and Interpretation*. Grand Rapids: Baker Academic, 2012.

Hooker, Morna D. *Paul: A Short Introduction*. Oxford: Oneworld, 2003.

Horrell, David G. *An Introduction to the Study of Paul*. Approaches to Biblical Studies. London: T&T Clark, 2000.

Longenecker, Bruce W., and Todd D. Still. *Thinking Through Paul: A Survey of His Life, Letters, and Theology*. Grand Rapids: Zondervan, 2014.

Meeks, Wayne A., and John T. Fitzgerald, eds. *The Writings of St. Paul*. 2nd ed. New York: W. W. Norton, 2007.

Westerholm, Stephen, ed. *The Blackwell Companion to Paul*. Malden, MA: Wiley-Blackwell, 2011.

Works on Romans

Byrne, Brendan, SJ. *Romans*. Sacra Pagina. Collegeville, MN: Liturgical Press, 1996.

Grieb, A. Katherine. *The Story of Romans: A Narrative Defense of God's Righteousness*. Louisville: Westminster John Knox, 2002.

Hultgren, Arland. *Paul's Letter to the Romans*. Grand Rapids: Eerdmans, 2011.

Keck, Leander E. *Romans*. Abingdon New Testament Commentaries. Nashville: Abingdon, 2005.

Matera, Frank J. *Romans*. Paideia Commentaries on the New Testament. Grand Rapids: Baker Academic, 2010.

Westerholm, Stephen. *Understanding Paul: The Early Christian Worldview of the Letter to the Romans*. 2nd ed. Grand Rapids: Baker Academic, 2004.

See also the notes in the chapters above for suggestions about specific topics and texts.

ANCIENT SOURCES INDEX

SUBJECT INDEX

Subject Index

136